Testimonials for *Mag*

"*Magnetic Love is the only kind of love there is, and Jennie has put this down in words better than anyone I've ever seen. It's a book you owe it to yourself to read and your library is incomplete without it. It holds the secret to the happiness in life*"

> ~ Bob Proctor
> Co-Founder, Proctor Gallagher Institute

"*The degree of our success in life is proportionate to our willingness to invest in learning. Love and gratitude are both powerful energies which ignite the passions that push us beyond all adversity and mediocrity.* Magnetic Love *is a remarkable must-read if you truly want to discover the greatness in YOU!*"

> ~ Les Brown, World's Leading Motivational Speaker

"*I met Jennie Lynn in December 2016 as we were both collaborating with Bob Proctor. A few months later here she is with a remarkable new book, Magnetic Love, endorsed by him. This book showcases her talents and devotion that will empower many people for a lifetime and is a transformational masterpiece the world has been aching for. It is a pleasure to have her join the Lurn Nation family to take her mission to the next level and ignite intellectual metamorphosis globally*".

> ~ Anik Singal, Lurn Nation Founder and
> Best Selling Author of *Circle of Profit*

"*My wish for you, and I know the author's wish for you, is only success... victory in loving yourself, happiness in your relationships, fulfillment in health, money freedom and anything else you desire. There is a goldmine of wisdom in this book, and it is time to start releasing the greatness that is within you.*"

> ~ Peggy McColl, *New York Times* Best-selling Author
> http://PeggyMcColl.com

"*In* Magnetic Love, *author Jennie Laurent, fellow Mentee of Bob Proctor has written the 'KEY' to unlocking the freedom you desire in all areas of life. Every paragraph of every chapter holds power in ways that I will be a applying for years to come.*"

> ~ William Todd, Author of *The Mentor In Me*

"*Magnetic Love is a magical journey of the most important love we can have – self-love! Allow Jennie to guide you through your awakening to the beautiful soul just waiting for you. You will learn a plethora of powerful lessons infused by personal stories to attract your deepest desires and feel in control of your life.* Magnetic Love *is a must-read!*"

~ Alena Chapman, Bestselling Author, Mentor & Speaker

"*Magnetic Love is a literary masterpiece that is both extraordinary and highly thought-provoking. Jennie Lynn is a brilliant and talented author, furnishing her readers with a captivating experience they will appreciate for a lifetime.*"

~ [Visionary] Bryan Smith

"*Magnetic Love will guide you through a spiritual journey of self-love, where you can't help but feel enlightened and empowered. In a world that is constantly trying to force us to be anything but real, Jennie shares her inspiring stories and life lessons on the necessity for us to freely be our authentic selves so we can unlock the gifts of abundance in life. The duality of love is that it is both simple yet profound. We all aspire to achieve happiness and peace of mind in life, and this remarkable book will show you the way.*"

~ Judy O'Beirn, Founder and Co-author of the International Best-selling Book Series *Unwavering Strength*

"*This is more than just a book, it's a gateway and a tool you can study and use to live the life of your dreams. You need to love yourself and be grateful for what you have, before you even consider asking for more. Jennie Lynn helps you make sense of your mind and teaches you all the things you didn't learn in school, but that will enrich your life and truly enlighten you.*"

~ Sandra L Gallagher
Proctor Gallagher Institute
CEO/Co-Founder

"*If you want to learn how to have success in every area of your life, then let Jennie Lynn inspire you to dream bigger and achieve more than you ever thought possible.*"

~ Steve Harrison, YourQuantumLeap.com

Magnetic Love

Stop Chasing What You Want...
Start Attracting It

– FOREWORD BY BOB PROCTOR –

by Jennie Lynn

Permission should be addressed in writing to Jennie Lynn:
PO Box 159, Lunenburg, MA 01462 or Jennielynn@jennielynn.com,
508-330-6217

Editor, Sigrid Macdonald
sigridmacdonald@rogerscom

Cover and Book Design, Anne Karklins
annekarklins@gmail.com

ISBN-13: 978-1-988071-41-1
ISBN-10: 1988071410

To my soulmate,
my partner in love forever, Brian Dalmaso

ABSTRACT

HOW AMAZING WOULD IT FEEL
TO FINALLY GET WHAT YOU'VE ALWAYS WANTED?

- Is it a loving, blissful relationship?

- Is it a youthful, healthy body?

- Is it enough money to live your life freely on your terms?

Whatever your deepest desire may be, if you don't have it yet, you need to stop winging it and start using science.

Understand that "like attracts like" and you interact with the world much like a magnet. Ignoring this fact has only repelled what you want most.

Jennie Lynn combines the latest research with the profound science of attraction. If you follow these proven methods, you will:

- Permanently remove the beliefs and habits blocking you from what you want

- Rewire your mind to draw love, health, & prosperity to you

- Explore what love really is so you know when you have found it

- Attract your soulmate and enhance your current love life

Don't settle for less or leave any of this to chance. Chasing is hard work, time consuming and offers no guarantee. *Magnetic Love* delivers a clear path that is definite, fast, and precise.

If you are seriously committed to your desires and dreams, you'll do whatever it takes. So take action now because nothing is more expensive than a missed opportunity. Love, fortune, and freedom await!

MEANING OF THE COVER DESIGN

This cover is highly symbolic and metaphorical because it combines many elements. When I was debating what to put on the cover, I wanted a striking concept, something impactful, and visually captivating. I worked carefully with my graphic artist, Anne Karklins, to design what I feel is a very conceptual and artistically appealing image of what this book conveys. The expression on my face is one of excitement, anticipation, and my look is slightly genie-like. As a prosperity coach, I demand the greatness that is in my client, because figuratively I invoke a butterfly when they are stuck in the cocoon.

I really liked the idea of an hourglass, in lieu of the magic lamp because it's all about time and how the sand flows downward, but I wanted to add my own twist. As Jennie the Love Genie, I help people and empower them to make their dreams and wishes come true. The book in the bottom chamber is symbolic of the magic of knowledge and universal laws. You can see that the energy is flowing from the book into the upper chamber creating the image of a heart, which represents the frequency of love. I was attracted to this concept because most people just go with the flow in life like sand through the hourglass, day after day. Certain people, though, live life purposefully and intentionally. We fight against the grain and create the lives we want and defeat all the odds that stand in our way. Love is a very powerful force, and we program our minds with the knowledge from the books we read. We also know that time is our most precious commodity in life and is as important, if not more important than money. You can always get more money, but you can never get more time, so we need to learn to invest it wisely and cherish it. The three most coveted goals in life are love, time and financial freedom.

My intention is that the knowledge you obtain through reading this book will help translate into a deeper understanding of who you really are as you discover your true self and fill your heart with love. This is truly the essential starting point to attract and receive *anything* you desire in life. If you ever struggle in life, remember this image and believe fiercely that love conquers all.

A Special Message from Jennie Lynn

Congratulations!

You have made a wonderful decision
to empower yourself and transform your life
through *Magnetic Love!*

Please ensure you take full advantage
of the amazing FREE BONUS GIFTS
that are being offered for a limited time
during/after the official Amazon launch.

Please visit
www.MagneticLove.com
NOW and enter your name, email,
and order # to retrieve
your free gifts and bonuses!

I am so excited and grateful to be a part of your journey.

With Love,
Jennie Lynn

FOREWORD

I've dedicated the past fifty years of my life to two things: (1) studying universal laws and (2) teaching people the art of living abundant lives. To that end, I've read thousands of books on the human mind, personal development and wealth building, written several books of my own, and held countless seminars around the world.

In December 2016, I met Jennie and her fiancé, Brian, at an elite Proctor Gallagher event. Jennie shared the story of how she and Brian had met, and I witnessed the excitement she emanated when she shared their unique story. I knew then that they were an influential and intimately connected couple.

Later, Jennie mentioned that she felt inspired to write a book highlighting their story and the lessons of her past. I encouraged her to pursue it.

Within two weeks, she let me know she had finished writing the book. I've met many aspiring authors in my lifetime who have a worthy story to tell; however, very few do anything to turn that dream into a reality. Her quick action demonstrates that, much like me, this young woman is serious and passionate about helping others.

In *Magnetic Love*, you'll see what can happen when you live in harmony with the universal laws which pave the way to success. Like my life, Jennie's story is a testament to how much your life can change when you immediately apply what you learn from books and mentors. The universe likes speed.

This inspirational and thought-provoking book will guide you through a challenging and introspective adventure of self-discovery. And nothing is more important than figuring out who and what you are as you walk your life's path.

Bob Proctor
Co-Founder, Proctor Gallagher Institute

INTRODUCTION

I am deeply grateful that my book has been divinely guided into your hands simply by your intention to elevate your life and harness the true power of yourself and love. I'm equally excited to help guide you to having not only a more loving relationship with yourself, but more importantly, how to master the power of your mind and soul to achieve fulfillment and a blissfully abundant life. Throughout this book, you will discover a similar pattern of synchronicities as you begin to learn and harness the incredible power within you to attract anything you desire like a magnet. We will be teaching you how to align yourself with the frequencies of your thoughts so that you are in harmony with what you desire. With a special focus on how to attract your soulmate, you will learn the essential prerequisites and *precisely* how to receive this and anything you desire in life. My whole life, all I ever wanted more than anything else was to meet my soulmate. But I experienced a great deal of frustration because unbeknownst to me, I was subconsciously blocking myself from getting what I wanted. The same issue may very well be blocking you from getting what you want too.

I learned that I needed to completely love myself and feel worthy and deserving of what I wanted or I could never get it. Once I realized what I was doing wrong while trying to use the law of attraction, I learned the real secret to unleashing its power. I really believed in these laws, and the evidence helped prove that this concept applies to attract anything you want. It really is not a secret; it's simply an art that you must learn and practice that is unique to you. It's often called "the secret" because few people know about it, let alone understand it enough to apply it optimally. I endeavor to change that by guiding you through this adventurous book and sharing my experiences with what I was doing wrong and what finally worked. I want you to feel the incredible power that is in you and how free you will feel when you're liberated from your burdens, and your path in life becomes clear. Everyone wants peace of mind and to just enjoy life doing what they want with who they want. You can have all of this and more! What you will read is so incredibly powerful, so I encourage you to focus and give this your undivided attention to achieve optimal results.

Almost all of us desire that deep connection with another human spirit so that we can share our lives with them and live in love forever. In my opinion, there is no greater feeling than to finally have my partner in life, someone who has my back, and someone I can depend on to live in harmony while sharing the best things in life together. Love is the most powerful force in the universe. When you have not found your soulmate in life and are asked what you desire, you would most likely answer "love," and all my life I answered the same. And love is exactly what I received; however, it was not the love I truly wanted and desired. Although I thought I was doing everything right, I was missing one critical element that would bring my *precise* desire to fruition. And for so long, I wished I knew why and what I was doing wrong. My parents loved me, my friends loved me, and I attracted men whom I thought loved me. I was either miserably single or in an unbalanced relationship. Each relationship provided a wonderful high, and I was so sure it would last forever only to have it fail time after time, leading to the doubt that I would ever find the man of my dreams. You see, all this time I kept thinking about love and doing everything I could do to get it; I craved and wanted it desperately. But the critical error that I made was mistaking love for infatuation – there is a very big difference.

However, I realized that it was not only *love* I was seeking, but it was my soulmate, my *partner*, and to be in intimate harmony with my "one and only." I hadn't specified this clearly enough. External love comes from others like friends and family, and I was surrounded by all this love, but what I desired was my romantic partner and monogamous soulmate. I discovered that love comes from within. I AM love, you ARE love, and love is what we give, not what we ask for. I needed to learn to love myself first and be exactly that which I desired and shift my energy and focus so that the universe would respond accordingly. Once I shifted my desire to focus on my eternal soulmate and not something as broad as "love," he walked right into my life. Our connection was instantly and wildly magnetic. When you meet your soulmate, you will know because you will experience a compelling force, a feeling of inseparability almost like a gravitational pull. It will be a natural high, unlike anything you have ever experienced or could imagine as you feel mutually unconditional acceptance and harmony. It will be an explosion of emotions, bewildering clarity, and a divine feeling of euphoria that empowers and enlivens you. It was not until I wrote my goals down, specified exactly what it is I wanted and attached a deadline to it that he showed up in my life almost effortlessly. And I wished I had known all along that it was so simple! Therefore, the mission of *Magnetic Love* is to help you and others learn from my mistakes so that you can avoid the unnecessary frustration I experienced and take the right actions to attract all your heart's desires NOW.

You may be tempted to skip ahead, but if you don't explore what the problem is, you will have a hard time applying the solution, so take this in stride and embrace the learning process. Throughout this book, you will learn what love really is, where we go wrong, and how to change our thinking and discover the power deep within us so that we can attract not only our soulmate but anything we desire in life. I am incredibly excited that you've made the choice to embark on this journey with me, as it will be both challenging and enigmatic. So I ask you to open your heart and your mind to this valuable information and not only read the words, but put them into action and bring this to life. Love is the greatest intangible gift and a language we all must learn to speak properly, so I am beyond privileged to be able to help guide you through this exhilarating journey so you can finally attract and receive everything you have ever desired. So without further ado, LET'S BEGIN!

TABLE OF CONTENTS

SECTION 1

LET'S BEGIN

CHAPTER 1

WHAT IS LOVE?

"Never forget that the most powerful force on earth is love."

~ Unknown

When we are asked what love is, most people would say that it's a strong and pleasant feeling. And that's entirely true. However, most people don't realize that the feelings and emotions we interpret as love are actually a response to us tuning into a particular frequency that is all around us in unlimited abundance. When we feel loved, or someone is sending us love, we feel joy and pleasure because they are sending positive energy that we are receiving. Love is inherent in all of us. Love is like oxygen; it's invisible and omnipresent like waves of sound that we cannot see, but they are always there.

Few people have ever experienced true love because it is complete and harmonious resonance and syncronicity between two people. Love is multi-dimensional and one of the few things humans can actually perceive that transcends all time and space. Love feels so good because connecting to that frequency releases chemical neuro-transmitters or "bonding hormones" like dopamine and oxytocin which creates that natural high feeling.

This may or may not be the first time you are introduced to the universal law of attraction. There are many universal laws, one of which is gravity, which I am certain you have heard of. Whether you believe in it or not, it is an invisible force all around us. If you jump off a bridge, whether you believe in gravity or not, you will fall. The law of attraction is no different, in that we are constantly attracting all the things and people into our lives. What you will learn throughout this book is that the law of attraction is a secondary law that responds to the law of vibration. To become a magnet for what we desire, we must learn how to be in control of the vibration we are in because it is our transmission with the universe and could attract either good or bad circumstances. Until you become consciously aware of such laws, you can then take advantage of how to tune into the right frequencies to attract only what you desire.

Similar to the law of cause of effect, when you give, you receive, and what you sow, you shall reap. Life is an echo of these forces, which is the law and cannot be denied. You see, our thoughts become energy waves that we constantly emit, which send out signals like a ripple effect into the universe. When we align ourselves in vibrational harmony with the frequency of love, we feel the pleasant feeling of what we interpret as loving energy. Love truly is a wonderful gift that we both give and receive but also what we embody. There are many forms of love, and what I desired most was to find my soulmate and live in unconditional devotion and spiritual harmony with him for eternity. We must learn that when we wholeheartedly love another, we do not try to change them to suit our needs, but we accept them unconditionally and express gratitude daily for the gift. Mastering the concept of love and attraction is a learning process, and we must explore where we may have picked up destructive habits or thought patterns so that we can truly receive what we desire most.

Love is very simple, yet we complicate it and this is often clouded by fear. When we remove the ego and get in tune with ourselves and our emotions, it should flow easily. When we come from a place of love and not fear, our intentions are pure and our thoughts and actions are parallel. It is a shame we were neither taught about love or our emotions in school. That is why so many people have this battle between their head and their heart. They don't understand themselves strongly enough to be able to understand another. We also bring all this stored up unresolved emotional baggage to new relationships only to repeat the same patterns and face the same consequences. Your results will reflect your inner thinking and as you raise your awareness, you will discover what you need to change so that you attract only what you want. We have five senses of taste, hear, smell, touch, and see. But the extra sense is the ability to feel, to interpret vibes and energy. We hear with our ears, but we listen with our emotions. We look through our eyes, but we are really seeing with our brain and cells of recognition from our past to interpret the present. Our subconscious mind is in control of 95% of our actions and decisions, and is emotionally driven. You may not understand why you think and do certain things because you're not really thinking, you're just exhibiting mental activity driven by the subconscious. Your beliefs are reflected in your outer reality, and again, you can change your reality and your results by changing your thoughts and paradigms which control your logic.

Through diligent study of who you really are, you will understand your true potential and what your greatest gifts are that you can offer another. You will realize that giving and receiving are one in the same and you will be able to cultivate happiness regardless of your outside circumstances. This is a learning process and a journey, so ensure that you have the right understanding and attitude about love. Remember that when we work in harmony with universal law and align our paradigms and vibration in harmony with universal law, our desires will flow to us. Your results will be your guide to how well you are manifesting and how aware you are. Keep your mind and heart open to the lessons you will receive as you embark on this path of enlightenment. It is the most liberating and fulfilling journey you can take in life.

> *"Love is not something we pursue;*
> *it's all around us and it is something*
> *we tune into through directed intention."*
> ~ *Jennie Lynn*

CHAPTER REFLECTION

Please take a moment at the end of this chapter to reflect on something that stood out to you. Record the greatest lessons you will want to remember so you can read these from time to time.

CHAPTER 2

A POWERFUL STORY OF A HEALING BREAKTHROUGH

"Today someone is going to hug you so tight that
all of your broken pieces will fall together.
That someone is you, yes. You're the only one who can.
So wrap your arms around yourself and make a habit of this
daily and watch how your life transforms."

~ Jennie Lynn

Along the journey of writing this book, I have experienced small shifts in my thinking as I incorporated more and more of Bob Proctor's teachings into my life and career. I've also noticed that the relationship I've had with myself has dramatically improved. This book was originally going to be more specific about love and how to find your soulmate. This was because once I learned to love myself, I found the love of my life. But I noticed that some unhealed wounds of my past began to surface as I relived and described some of the lowest and most painful moments of my life. It has expanded into a magical story of self-healing, self-love, deep introspection, and deeper understanding about the universal laws than I've ever known as I raised my conscious awareness. It truly reminded me how far I have come.

What struck me once I finished the book is that I am not the same person that I was when I started writing it. I love myself now more than I ever have in my life, and I experienced almost a miraculous healing. I think you will enjoy the happy ending of my story and feel many of you may resonate with and learn from some of my struggles.

I will take you back to 2012 when I decided to get into body-building and fitness modeling with a goal to earn my pro card and make it big. To make a long story short, after sixteen weeks of a grueling diet and training regimen, I hit the stage for my first competition, and I didn't even place. I told myself that I would never put myself through that again, and so I continued to resume my normal life and just do modeling. After months of rebound, and my body rebelling for the few months I put it through hell, my health took a nose dive.

As a nurse, I knew something was wrong, and after months of trying to fix it, I wound up stressed out, exhausted, and ten pounds heavier than when I started competing. I found a naturopathic doctor who recognized this, and after some diagnostics, I was diagnosed with a very debilitating thyroid disorder called Hashimoto's, which is an autoimmune form of an under active thyroid. I had just gotten in the best shape of my life, and it had quickly been taken away from me, and I fell deep into almost a depression because I was not myself. I was tired and frustrated, hated the way I looked, and completely lost.

It took four years for me to research this condition and try to get myself back to at least a healthy weight and feeling like myself. Because I still had that goal of turning pro in my mind, I had the urge to give the stage another shot. It took me two more tries, but I finally earned my first pro card in late 2014 in the figure category, and this was probably one of the proudest moments in my life.

I went on to compete as a pro for the first time two weeks later, and I won pro figure, and also a second pro card in physique. The momentum kept building, and the following year I did the same thing and won a third pro card in body-building, and it was an "on top of the world" kind of feeling. I got used to winning, but you can't always win. Also, I knew

I was walking a fine line with my health, and it again began to decline. But this time I knew better, and although it was difficult to walk away from a passion, I would not make the same mistake twice and jeopardize my health.

In summer of 2016, I officially retired as a professional competitor. However, it was challenging to assimilate back to a "normal" life, when I was so accustomed to adhering to a strict diet, perfecting my stage presence, and following a rigorous exercise regimen. I realized that I was clinging to something I thought I had full control over, but it was really controlling me. I found what I thought was balance, but I still had a negative relationship with myself, the gym, and food. I almost just accepted that this was the way it was going to have to be. For years I had immersed myself in trying to find a cure for this "disease," following every guru, but I was fighting a losing battle with weight gain and fatigue, which is a bodybuilder and model's worst nightmare. I searched high and low for natural cures and researched different diets. I managed the best way I knew how, but I was searching for answers outside of myself, looking for the right doctor, diet, or supplement that would help me feel normal again.

Fast forward to February 2017; it was as if overnight all of those little shifts I had been making all came together, and I woke up the morning of the 19th and had more energy than I have ever had; I felt like a kid again and had such clairvoyance! I didn't see this coming, and it was a feeling of simultaneous peace and vitality and freedom. This was in stark contrast to the crippling fatigue I had been battling for years after being diagnosed with the thyroid condition.

I realized that for the first time in my life, I really loved myself and those seeds of love I had been planting recently had finally grown. I discovered that I was my own best friend, and it was amazing to see how a shift in my perception made me see myself and my life in a completely different way that helped me let go of all those vices. It was like meeting who I really was for the first time as I had been chasing a perfect image of who I thought I wanted to be, but that was not who I was, that was the old me.

When you begin to understand what an autoimmune disease is, you will find that it means the body starts to attack itself. What I learned was that my poor self-image and self-criticism was causing a battle inside my body, and I felt powerless over it. I had immersed myself so much in this disease that I was subsequently ignoring what it was trying to tell me. For years my body had been screaming at me to STOP and pay attention.

I realized that I had abused my body quite a bit, not ever thanking it for all the wonderful things it does for me and appreciating myself. I developed a very negative and unhealthy relationship with food and the gym that controlled my life and left me chasing perfectionism. Because I didn't love myself and I was not perfect according to my unrealistic standards, I became disconnected, and my soul suffered. My body was telling me something, and because I didn't understand what it was saying, I could not listen. I also had a narrow and limited thought process that was blocking me, and I was completely oblivious to the damage I was causing until my health was failing so much it demanded my attention.

Once I raised my conscious awareness and started to learn to love myself and discover who I really was, I experienced the most significant breakthrough in my life so far. I realized that I needed to stop fighting myself and end this internal battle that was robbing me of my health. Every time I ate, I never felt satisfied and had deprived myself of pleasurable foods so that I could maintain a perfect body. While I interpreted this as a ravenous appetite and hunger for food, my body was really starving for LOVE. My body needed me to nurture myself and heal all the wounds, and for the first time in my life, I felt in control, and I realized that what is most important is what I feed my mind. Food was just a Band-Aid, but the hunger never went away because I didn't get the message from my body to heal yet. But all the answers and everything I needed were always within me. I finally realized what my body was telling me, and that disease exists as feedback to what we need to change internally to get to the root of a problem. I had been reciting healing affirmations every morning, and this one morning changed my life because I felt healed and full of life. I told myself that I was free of disease and that I loved myself, flaws and all.

When I stopped focusing on the disease, the disease ceased to exist, and as I nurtured myself with love, my body began to heal, and I shed all the layers and burdens of the past and forgave myself for hurting me for so long. I always believed in self-healing, but again I never knew how, and this was the first time feeling it, how real it was, and it made me a believer. I had finally discovered the deep reservoirs of love within myself, and that nothing external can heal me or hurt me, because what happens in my mind is what creates my reality, and when I changed my thinking, my life changed miraculously. Now that I have heard my body and soul speak to me, I now listen to everything it tells me and continue to evolve and connect on an even deeper level.

Though I wish I never had to go through that pain, it offered valuable lessons I will never forget. Growing pains are necessary in life because as much as I was tempted to quit or crawl up in a ball of self-pity and self-loathing depression, I have a strong inner conscience that keeps me fighting. While this was a battle I needed to win on my own, I do attribute much of my healing and revelations to the unwavering and tremendous love and support of my amazing soul mate, Brian. He is and always has been the wind beneath my wings. Failure or quitting was never an option for me because I am like ants because when faced with any obstacle, they defy science with their strength. I am now fearless, limitless, and so full of love and life that I just want to inspire others how to heal their relationship with themselves so they can have flourishing relationships with others and a truly abundant life.

What excites me the most is that reading my own book after writing it caused an even more powerful transformation than I had ever experienced. That is the power of love! You have witnessed my incredible story of self-discovery, and how loving myself helped me become a magnet for healing, abundance, my soulmate, and virtually every desire I have ever wanted. My intention is that you believe in miracles and how this can happen for you as you connect to your higher self. It is a learning process and a journey, and I know that once you get the slightest bit of evidence that your efforts are manifesting, you will become invincible. You will discover those deep reservoirs of love and believe you can achieve anything you want and attract anything you desire when you first create yourself as the magnet and fill yourself with love.

"Your purpose on this earth is not to do, but rather to be.
Because you are not what you do.
Expand and amplify your true potential and bring it to the surface.
Embrace your highest self."

~ Jennie Lynn

What I would like to now share with you is what made me spring up out of bed at 3 am that morning that I wrote this because the idea popped right into my head, and I didn't want to waste any time manifesting this while I was in tune with the energy. I had officially finished writing this book, but it would not be complete without adding this afterthought. It dawned on me that this is how I know I am following my passion in life. It's what motivates me to leap out of bed like a child on Christmas Day because I can't wait to start my day and experience the gifts of life and manifest my dreams. Almost my whole life, I've had a broken relationship with myself unknowingly until just recently, which was cultivated by a perfectionist paradigm.

Every time I used to look in the mirror, my eyes would focus right on my flaws, and this became a daily habit. It's almost like I was so unhappy with my reflection, I one day said to myself that maybe I should just stop looking in the mirror. I thought how silly that would be to go through life avoiding mirrors. But it got me to think that the only time I really focused on my "flaws" was when I looked at myself in the mirror. I wondered if this is what people saw when they looked at me. It was that bad habit of looking in the mirror and only seeing a reflection of an imperfect person because that's what I kept telling myself that I was. And we believe what we tell ourselves.

I had recently made a new friend, [Visionary] Bryan Smith, who is an expert in the law of attraction, and I told him all about my book. He told me about a daily ritual of his that I should try. He told me to wake up and look in the mirror and talk to myself; look deep into my eyes and ask the universal source (God) to empower me to help others, and after doing this repeatedly, I would meet my higher self. I tried it a few times and thought it would be cool if it really worked. Then I came across a quote that stated, "If only our eyes saw souls instead of bodies, how different our idea of beauty might be." And then it hit me. I finally realized what I had been doing wrong all my life, and what I needed to do to fix it; I finally found "the cure" – I call it the mirror miracle.

I had nearly resigned myself to the fact that I was going to have to manage my autoimmune thyroid disease the best way I knew how and that I was just going to have to live with it. But throughout the course of writing this book and implementing the knowledge I had been immersing myself in, I realized what I had been doing wrong. My eyes could not see what my mind could not comprehend, and I could not hear my body's plea for help to stop the perfectionist sabotage. But for the first time, it became crystal clear! It was as if I had finally found that last missing puzzle piece of self-love to complete a picture of me so that I met my real self for the first time.

I had been habitually ungrateful for my body, feeling incomplete, and unloving of myself. I was expecting the universe to grant me everything I desired, and I got frustrated when it would not manifest. What I discovered is that I was operating off a frequency of *lack* where I was trying to manifest a desire of *abundance*. These are two opposing frequencies, and unless the source is in harmony with the desire, the two cannot connect; it's like oil and water. When I finally shifted my thinking and loved myself, I experienced this miraculous healing.

This became the premise of the title of my book, and how we need first to become the magnet for what we desire so we can connect in harmony with it using the law of attraction. I loved the title *Magnetic Love*, but I did not fully understand its deeper meaning until I was done writing my book and experienced the incredible power of it myself! How powerful is it that I can change my reality simply by changing my thoughts! A major light bulb went on, and this has changed my life forever.

A smile is contagious, and what better way to start my day than to wake up and look in the mirror and see my soul smiling back at me because I love who I am. It is so amazing now to love who I see in the mirror when only weeks before this, I was a stranger to myself. What an amazing transformation my life underwent simply because I finally was able to change the perception I had of myself. I cannot convey in words how ingratiating it is that I completely love myself and am finally healed. I realize how, for half my life, I wasted so much energy on criticizing myself that I caused my own health to decline, and this destruction was blocking the abundance and freedom I craved. Our bodies know how to heal, but we are often the cause of our diseases because of the stress we put on ourselves and how we perceive life which disconnects us, weakens us, and sabotages our health. Even with the perfect diet and exercise regimen, that wasn't enough for me to heal until I removed the perfectionist stress.

The only way to truly heal is to fully discover and love who we are, and take the necessary actions to manifest healing. It was only when I stopped focusing on and talking about the disease and trying to force myself into healing that I learned that focusing on the disease only perpetuated more of it. When I began to focus on self-love and affirming I was already healed, I witnessed my own miracle and connected myself to the cure of self-love. We can only heal when we fully believe that this is possible.

I am so amazed at how elevating my conscious awareness allowed me to speak to my soul and finally hear what my body has been trying to communicate to me for years. I am so grateful that because of my desire to write this book to help others, the universe rewarded me with the ability to help myself heal, something I had been chasing for years. This made me understand the law of giving and receiving more than ever.

I cannot think of a better way to share this experience with the world than by writing a book, and my dream is to help inspire others to be able to heal and love themselves and understand the incredible power of the mind and the soul. Every time you look in the mirror, realize that you choose what you want to see, so smile back at yourself because you're beautiful, just like my good friend [Visionary] Bryan Smith always says. As you read on, I invite you to embrace a more loving relationship with yourself, which will enrich your current and future relationships. You will discover that this book is about so much more than love and relationships. I am confident that you will come to the realization that once you align your heart with your mind, your world will manifest into the wonderful reality that deep down you've always wanted but that has been just out of reach, until now.

Jennie's HEALING AFFIRMATIONS

My body was created by the universal intelligence in my subconscious mind. It intuitively knows how to heal me. Every atom of my being was created by this infinite wisdom.

I welcome the healing presence within me that is now unfolding, creating my complete and pristine self.

I am deeply grateful for the healing I know is now taking place.

I am fascinated by the handiwork of the universal intelligence within me.

I know I am now perfectly healthy and healed. Being healthy is and always has been my natural state of existence.

My mind has the power to heal my body now. My eternal spiritual soul is now healing me.

I now return to this natural state of perfect health.

My mind and body has the infinite potential to heal me now. My body and mind are now unconditionally healed and healthy.

My body, spirit, soul and mind are united with the universal intelligence.

My body, spirit, soul, and mind have the ability to heal me now.

I am now in a state of perfect health and I am healed spiritually, physically, mentally, and emotionally. I now remove any hindrance to my natural state of healing and health.

Every fiber of my being was created by the universe intelligence in my subconscious mind. It has always healed me and is healing me now as I embrace my perfect health. I am so happy and grateful for this healing.

If you would like access to the audio/video version as well as a special exercise I created you can practice daily that allowed me to heal myself, please visit www.themirrormiracle.com and opt in to receive this free gift – It also includes my power-point slides so you can print this out and tape it to your mirror like I did!

CHAPTER REFLECTION

Please take a moment at the end of this chapter to reflect on something that stood out to you. Record the greatest lessons you will want to remember so you can read these from time to time.

CHAPTER 3

HOW DID WE LEARN HOW TO LOVE?

"In life, we are not so much becoming who we are meant to be, but rather coming home to who we really are"

~ Jennie Lynn

From the moment of conception at a cellular level, you began receiving signals about love and growth. You were fed nutrients from your mother, and depending on the environment, whether you were given proper nutrients or surrounded by poor nourishment or toxins, this impacted your growth. At birth, we are totally dependent beings, so receiving love and having our needs met from our parents is imperative. When you are born and until the age of about seven, your body and brain are still developing, and your mind is like a sponge soaking up everything all around you. We have two minds, a subconscious mind which we cannot control and a conscious mind which we can.

As children, we are controlled by our subconscious, and this part of our mind cannot reject; it must accept. So whatever we learn and experience as a child forms the foundation of our belief system. Children develop behaviors based on what they see, similar to the "monkey see, monkey do" analogy. Most people do not even realize the enormous power that our environment has over our lives. Have you ever heard the saying by Jim Rohn, "You are the average of the five people you spend the most time with"? This is entirely true as our environment shapes us, and energy is contagious, good or bad! You may have heard someone say, for example, that "misery loves company." Miserable people are overwhelmed by negative emotions, and they will share it with anyone who allows them. You should avoid being around such people, or you will end up sharing their energy and attitude.

I wanted to share another powerful example of the impact our environment can have on our lives. In 2010, a professor named Bruce Alexander conducted an experiment with a rat park to determine the potential for its impact on addiction. Bruce wanted to compare the drug consumption of rats in a normal playful environment to those in solitary confinement. On one side, Bruce replicated a fun, socially friendly place for the rats to mingle with unlimited access to morphine water. The other side was an isolation chamber where the rat was by itself with access to unlimited sources of morphine water. The results were astonishing. What Bruce and his team observed was that the rats in confinement drank much more morphine water, whereas the rats in the park almost ignored the morphine water.

"The view of addiction from Rat Park is that today's flood of addiction is occurring because our hyper individualistic, hyper competitive, frantic, crisis-ridden society makes most people feel social and culturally isolated. Chronic isolation causes people to look for relief. They find temporary relief in addiction to drugs or any of a thousand other habits and pursuits because addiction allows them to escape from their feelings, to deaden their senses, and to experience an addictive lifestyle as a substitute for a full life."

The rats in the park had as much access to the addicting solution as the rats that were isolated, but because they were preoccupied with a satisfying environment, they had little interest in an addicting substance. As humans, we live in a very similar set up in our environment in that our limited thinking becomes an invisible cage that we become a prisoner of. When we isolate ourselves or feel isolated, we lose control and become vulnerable to outside influences. Most people look for an outlet to dull the pain they cannot face, and this leads to addictions. We must ensure that if we are ever going to thrive and pursue our dreams, we must have a healthy and loving relationship with ourselves and surround ourselves with others who are loving and supportive.*

In the next section of this book, we will delve deeper into just how powerful the mind is. It is incredible the amount of influence that things like movies, books, music, television, and the media have on our perceptions. If you watch movies about love and listen to songs of joy, and your parents provided a loving environment and encouraging affirmations, you are bound to have a strong connection to loving energy.

Conversely, if you listen to songs about heartache and hate, and watch violent movies or dramatic soap operas, and grow up in a neglectful environment, you are not likely to thrive and perceive the loving energy needed to flourish. Your belief system and behaviors will reflect the negative patterns you were exposed to, and this will continue into adulthood until you learn to reject those belief systems and create new ones. We are creatures of habit, and we are often so accustomed to our habits that we are completely unaware of them. Sadly, love is not something we are taught in school, but it is a critical skill we need to master if we ever want to attract a loving and lasting relationship with ourselves and others.

> *"Educating the mind without educating the heart*
> *is no education at all."*
>
> *~ Aristotle*

There are only two emotions from which we operate that all other feelings can be categorized. These are love and fear. Most of us who have not discovered that deep level of awareness end up acting mostly out of fear and instinct. For example, each breakup I experienced led to deep pain and heartache. With each new relationship, I would not allow myself to open up or be vulnerable out of the fear of getting hurt. That is the absolute wrong mindset to be in because I was subconsciously putting up barriers to receiving the love I craved! Each failed relationship caused emotional scars and unreconciled baggage that I carried with me to each new relationship only to continue to repeat the same pattern of failure.

When I shifted my thinking, dialed in my focus, and learned this deep level of awareness, I was finally able to liberate myself from that vicious cycle. Remember that in order for you to receive *anything* you want in life, not just love, you need to believe in your own worth and love yourself first. Throughout this book you will learn the immense power of the mind, what drives our emotions, and how to take conscious control over this so that you are attracting only what you truly desire.

"To fully receive love and abundance, we must tune into
the frequency through intention and a deep emotional connection,
which by virtue removes any blocks to getting our deepest desires."

~ Jennie Lynn

* http://www.brucekalexander.com/articles-speeches/rat-park/148-addiction-the-view-from-rat-park

CHAPTER REFLECTION

Please take a moment at the end of this chapter to reflect on something that stood out to you. Record the greatest lessons you will want to remember so you can read these from time to time.

CHAPTER 4

LOVE MANIFESTS IN MANY FORMS

"In Life, we have many things that come in pairs, but there is
a reason why we only have one heart – and that is so we can truly
devote ourselves romantically to one person, our true soulmate."

~ Jennie Lynn

I previously mentioned that I thought love is what I desired, and as humans, we all want to be loved, adored, and appreciated. I was asking for love, and the universe responded by sending people who loved me and things I could love. I finally learned that to attract my soulmate, this was a special frequency of love I needed to specify. Love comes in so many forms and can be expressed in many different ways. We can love a person or an object, or we can be *in love*. You can be attracted to a person on purely a physical level. For example, we can find someone physically appealing and fall for him or her; however, this is lust and should not be confused with love.

We must understand that we are not our bodies. We are the souls within, and our body is just an avatar we live in. I remember in my adolescence, I was attracted to men almost purely on a physical level. I saw someone who was handsome or charming, and there was definitely an attraction. If we felt an attraction to one another, this is often called "chemistry." As adolescents, our brains are not fully formed, and we think we know what love is, but we are merely acting on emotions. That is why we have to go through a period of trial and error with relationships to help teach us who we are and what we are really looking for. I would be in a relationship with someone, and we would say we loved each other and express those sentiments. However, if the relationship ended, it was not meant to be. That does not mean it was not love, just that the love transcended to a different frequency. Your love for a friend is different than your love for a romantic partner. There are many ways people express love for a person even without saying it.

Throughout our lives, we come to understand what love is and what it is not. We meet people who use us or hurt us, but it ultimately teaches us how to recognize the frequency of true love. Most people are afraid of relationships like I was because I feared getting hurt and the relationship ending. When this is what you focus on, this is exactly what you will attract. You must understand that you need to shift your thinking to focus on only what you want, not what you fear or do not want.

The universe responded to my desire for love by sending me relationship after relationship, and each time I continued a cycle of falling in and out of what I thought was love. I kept thinking each person was my soulmate, and when I found out they were not, I was often confused and discouraged. I had to realize that I was also projecting my expectations onto others. Shakespeare stated that "expectation is the root of all heartache." It's okay to have fantasies and desires, but having unrealistic or unfair expectations can have unfavorable consequences. Everybody expresses love in different ways and for different reasons. You cannot force or demand love; it must flow freely and naturally. You can't expect everyone else to love the same way you do.

I wasted a lot of time wondering why this kept happening. But this was merely a learning process. I wondered if I was being too picky or not having a realistic idea of what a relationship was and I began to doubt if I would ever find it. I eventually learned that I was attracting the wrong frequency because I was not being specific about exactly what I desired, and I did not know or understand this concept. I repeated many mistakes until something finally clicked. I had to experience this many times before I finally learned the lesson the universe was communicating to me. I understood why I wasn't meeting my soulmate because even though I wanted to find him, I was not ready or worthy yet.

I read many books about love and how to be a good partner, and this was not enough. For me to truly maximize the law of attraction, I needed first to know exactly what I wanted in a partner, almost as if I were placing an order with the universe. I needed to write this down over and over so that it was clear to me and then clear to the universe. A common mistake people make is that they desire something but do not fully believe they can attract it. Wishing and hoping is not enough. I needed to banish such doubt, learn to love myself and believe with every fiber of my being that I would meet my soulmate.

Once I finally learned that very valuable lesson, it was a turning point in my life because I shifted my focus not on getting love but on attracting my soulmate. I was not aware of certain mental barriers and habits I had also formed that were destructive and hindering the delivery of what I truly wanted. In the next section, we will explore these further so that you can discover and shift what is holding you back.

"Someone once said that the best medicine for humans is love.
And if it does not appear to be working, simply increase the dose."

~ *Anonymous*

CHAPTER REFLECTION

Please take a moment at the end of this chapter to reflect on something that stood out to you. Record the greatest lessons you will want to remember so you can read these from time to time.

_____

_____

_____

_____

_____

_____

_____

_____

_____

_____

_____

_____

_____

_____

_____

_____

_____

_____

_____

_____

_____

_____

_____

CHAPTER 5

LOVE STARTS WITH YOU

"Your relationship with yourself ultimately sets the standard
for every other relationship in life. Love yourself, and you
will attract those who love you. Do not tolerate any less than
what you know you deserve."

~ *Jennie Lynn*

I will be the first to admit that I was wrongfully seeking love outside of myself in a desperate attempt to fill a self-love void. I felt incomplete and wanted to meet a man who would love me and who I could love. Deep down inside, I despised myself, I was not perfect, and I was insecure in my body. I was not aware then of these negative thoughts and energy I was sending out to the universe. In the midst of me wanting and needing, the universe responded to my frequency of that energy, leaving me in a constant state of wanting and needing. I was stuck and frustrated and discouraged!

I wanted love, but I did not consciously believe I deserved it because I didn't even love myself. How could anyone possibly love a person who does not love themselves? You cannot give what you don't have, no matter how much you convince yourself to believe this. This expectation that I needed to be loved to feel worthy and complete was ultimately keeping me in this emotional prison.

Wanting and needing someone to love me was entirely selfish, unattractive and, unbeknown to me, was attracting other people who didn't love me either. I also realized in retrospect that the people I was attracting were merely a reflection of my broken identity paradigm frequency – they were mirroring me. This is why relationship after relationship failed. I kept thinking I was attracting what I wanted, but I was settling for only what I felt I deserved. I would get mad at the universe for not sending it to me and question why, and once I realized I needed to love myself first and believe in my own worth, I was able to break that pattern. I blamed everyone but myself while justifying that I was doing everything right. In reality, I was the one doing it all wrong, and once I accepted that and became aware of these negative patterns, I was able to completely shift my thinking so that I could tune into the right frequencies. It was such an eye-opening experience to be awakened to and aware of these universal laws and forces. Instead of being controlled by a storm of emotions, once I raised my conscious awareness, I was able to think outside of myself and feel in control so I would respond instead of reacting. One of the most valuable lessons in life is to learn the art of remaining calm in any situation so that you're always collected and in control and never disillusioned by your emotions.

You've probably heard many people say that they are their own worst enemy or their own worst critic. This is simply a paradigm you must change immediately if you ever want to have the results in life that you desire. The core of our being, our source, must be one of positivity. We have to love ourselves and be our own best friend in life. We must be completely comfortable with who we are, physically, spiritually, and emotionally if we ever expect to connect with our goals in life. For example, you will see a lot of people in life who are overweight trying to lose weight. They are unhappy with their bodies, but despite their greatest attempts, they can never hate themselves thin. Additionally, if you are trying to get in shape but view exercise as a chore or punishment for overindulging in food, this is a very negative and completely counterproductive mindset to have.

Think of how much resistance you will meet every time you have to force yourself to do this – we always shy away from stressful stimuli. That is why you see people quit the healthy and fit lifestyle and fall back into bad habits. They think it's too difficult when in reality it's their mindset that is the problem, and therefore, they get undesirable results. Results do not lie, and what is going on inside of us is always reflected on the outside. We gravitate toward things that make us feel good, so if someone succeeds in dedicating themselves to a healthy lifestyle, they need to make a positive association with it. An example of this would be to make it a fun and collaborative activity, one that makes you feel good and that you can share with others.

It is essential to develop a positive self-image so that we are radiating with positivity because after all, we attract what we are. We should not love ourselves to the point of conceit, but we must silence that inner critic in ourselves and also pay no mind to the outside influences of society that we must look and act a certain way. We cannot shame and hate ourselves when we make mistakes. We need to make peace and learn to forgive ourselves and embrace our imperfections.

I remember that I used to care so much what other people thought of me. It was a really bad habit I developed because I was trying so hard to be accepted and please everyone. I ended up losing myself in the process and disconnecting with who I was because I was basing my self-worth on outside influences. It was an incredibly liberating feeling when I realized how destructive this was to my self-image and that I did not need to please anyone.

I pondered why I cared so much in the first place. It was because I was acting out of my subconscious, which was driven by societal pressure to be perfect. How silly it was that I was expecting myself to be perfect when no one else is or can be. I was resisting my body's desire to just be my real authentic self, and quite frankly, I had become a stranger to my soul. It was such a liberating feeling to connect with and discover who I really was, more than just my name and my body, but deep down in my soul. It breaks my heart to see so many people who have body dysmorphia or eating disorders because I've struggled with that myself.

You may be wondering right now if you are very critical of yourself like I was, how do you stop? There is no quick fix, but if you're dedicated to the results you want, you'll do what it takes. You need to reaffirm over and over to yourself the consequences of having a negative self-image. It causes all sorts of negativity that impacts your whole body, every single cell. It weakens your immune system, makes you ill, and puts you in a bad vibration, meaning you will attract all the things you don't want. What I found most helpful to building a positive self-image is to spend a little time every day writing down my ideal body, while visualizing in my mind what I would look like. How would I feel in that body?

Write this all down in a journal daily and watch how your body changes. You need to express gratitude for all the things about your body. Start writing a list. You will feel an amazing sense of peace when you start focusing on all the good your body does for you, as opposed to all your "imperfections." We often overlook all of our blessings our body comes with because we are focusing on what we are lacking, and we stay in a state of discontent with ourselves and our bodies in a vicious cycle. When you express gratitude for what you already have, the universe will reward you with more things to be thankful for. What we feed our bodies has an impact on how we feel, so by eating healthy, nutritious food, we are respecting our body as a temple, and this gives us the energy we need to think clearly and have a healthy body.

When our bodies are vibrantly healthy, we can focus on loving ourselves and feeling confident and invincible. When we feel good about ourselves, people take notice because we are vibrating on a positive frequency, and people gravitate toward those who make them feel good. This is the magnetic attraction you create when you connect deeply with yourself and love who you are. Most people focus only on what they want to manifest, and when it fails, they don't understand why. A good analogy of this is that if you don't first create yourself as the magnet for what you want; it's like throwing a broken boomerang. Boomerangs are designed to always come back to who threw them, and if it is broken, it will not return to you.

The core of our being is much like the core of the earth creating magnetic and gravitational pulls. For the law of attraction to work, we need to invest in becoming the magnet, and then the manifestation will come because we created the connection. There can be no effect without a cause. We can become a magnet for love, peace, abundance, health, wealth, joy, and anything we want in life. In subsequent chapters, you will discover more about the power of your mind and how to develop your unique magnetic forces that will connect you to your desires, and this all begins with love.

Our bodies are such an amazing phenomenon. Have you ever stopped and considered how amazing it is that your heart beats without you ever having to tell it to? Have you ever thanked your body for all the protection it provides for you and how it has healed all your wounds? It may sound silly, but we are so busy and stuck in our minds to truly appreciate our beauty. It is necessary to love and care for our bodies to nourish our souls. It blows my mind how I mindlessly pursued perfectionism to the point that I overlooked all the positive things I should love about myself, and in turn neglected to appreciate my body. I know now why I was suffering, but I was so blinded and did not understand it in the thick of things, and I was lost, and my mind was an angry storm. The constant criticism wore away at my self-esteem, and I was stuck in a skewed identity paradigm. Understand that your relationship with yourself ultimately sets the tone for every other relationship in your life. When you treat yourself poorly, others will too because that is the energy you are emitting.

When you establish a healthy and loving relationship with yourself, you create the standard for how others will treat you. When you truly learn to love yourself at even a cellular level and refuse to tolerate anything less than what you feel you deserve, you will attract people who love and cherish you. You will feel deserving and worthy of all that you ask of the universe, and you will learn how to be very specific with your request so you can connect to the right frequencies that deliver it to you. It is such an incredible phenomenon. The mistake most people make is that they try to walk before they learn to crawl, and they fail and get discouraged. So many people have been introduced to the secret and the law of attraction.

However, it is different to know what something is, but it's an entirely different game to be able to master it. The power is in knowledge, action, and belief. Throughout this book, you will learn how to crawl before you walk and understand the mental faculties you have so that you can master your craft. Our paradigms and fears keep us caged and stuck in our minds which create a vicious cycle of desperation in search for answers our souls seek. This is why we need help from others, because you have the wings, and I will teach you how to fly! There is no greater investment you can make than to invest in YOU and educate your mind and heart. You need to understand that your cup is full, never half full or half empty. It is only when you accept this and become so overflowing with love and abundance that you can truly share this with others.

"It is not through others that our worth is validated, but rather, we define our worth and attract a partner who is worthy"

~ Jennie Lynn

Jennie's CHECK YOURSELF CHECKLIST

1. Do I love myself? _____

2. Do I understand what love is and why I want it? _____

3. Do I feel happy and complete or am I looking for love to feel that way? _____

4. Do I know or am I willing to find out what my bad habits are and change them? _____

5. Do I feel that I am emotionally intelligent and a good communicator? _____

6. Do I know exactly what I want in another person and do I possess those qualities? _____

7. Do I often get too attached to people and fall apart after a break up or am I willing to accept it wasn't meant to be? _____

8. Do I feel I often get what I don't want and don't know why? _____

9. Do I see any good or bad patterns from past relationships? _____

On a scale from 1-10 how great of a lover am I and am I willing to accept responsibility for all that I attract into my life and not place blame? _____

CHAPTER REFLECTION

Please take a moment at the end of this chapter to reflect on something that stood out to you. Record the greatest lessons you will want to remember so you can read these from time to time.

_____

_____

_____

_____

_____

_____

_____

_____

_____

_____

_____

_____

_____

_____

_____

_____

_____

_____

_____

_____

_____

_____

SECTION 2

THE POWER OF YOUR MIND

CHAPTER 1

PARADIGMS: WHY WE GET STUCK

"If you realized how powerful your thoughts are,
you would never allow or entertain negative thoughts."

~ *Jennie Lynn*

In previous chapters, I made reference to destructive thought patterns and bad habits I had created subconsciously that were a major hindrance to me receiving what I really wanted. I will be teaching you that about 95 percent of the time, we are operating off our paradigms, which are heavily rooted in our subconscious, most of which we don't even have control over. In school, we are taught only about the conscious mind and how to learn information. We are taught about the brain anatomy, but we are not taught about consciousness and energy. I am going to show you step by step how to rewrite new beliefs into your subconscious so that you can experience the necessary shift to align yourself with the frequency so that you can take control and change your life. Until I realized this myself, I was repeating the same cycle of frustration and in constant wonder of what I might be doing wrong or questioning whether this law of attraction really works. Does that sound familiar?

Do you ever feel the same in that you think you're doing everything right and have the right attitude and therefore should be receiving what you truly want? If that is the case, then you have come to the right place to get the answers you seek. It delights me so much to be able to deliver this priceless information to you so that you can triumph over your own unique paradigms and learn how to live life on purpose and no longer be a prisoner of your destructive thought patterns and barriers to success.

You may be wondering what a paradigm is, and most people have never even heard of this concept before. A paradigm is a deep rooted belief, or a habit, or a vice that we have that drives our actions and our thinking. We learn some paradigms from our parents, in school, and from society. We think we are consciously aware of and in control of our thoughts and decisions but realize that we have two parts of our mind. One is the conscious mind, and the other is the subconscious mind. The subconscious mind cannot reject; it must accept, so whatever we experience or read or see or reaffirm gets written into this part of our mind. We don't have control over this, but what we can do is take action so that we can speak to this part of our mind and change those paradigms with more constructive thoughts and ideas. Be careful of something known as confirmation bias whenever you are learning something. You need to keep an open mind and understand that your paradigm will not allow you to consider ideas that contradict your beliefs. Allow yourself to be open to all the evidence around an idea and learn to persist beyond the resistance you may face from your paradigms. This is a process and requires a great deal of focus and repetition, and you will often experience a great deal of resistance as you fight your own beliefs.

"The universe will repeat the lesson until it is learned."

~ *Jennie Lynn*

Take a look at your life. Do you make the kind of money you want? Are you surrounded by like-minded and positive people? Do you feel like you're achieving your goals? Your paradigm will do everything in its power to keep you locked in your comfort zone, and it will take a great deal of courage to confront deeply ingrained beliefs. It will be uncomfortable as you face those inner demons and your fears surface and plead with you to retreat! I want you to be prepared for this and expect this and know that it is totally normal but also imperative that you persist beyond these feelings. Our conscious mind influences only a small fraction of our mind and is synonymous with awareness. Do you ever wonder why we do what we do? Do you wonder why or how we do some things we know we should not do but we do them anyway? Or why we fail to do what we know we should do? There is only a small window when the answers are revealed to us that we can ACT on them before our paradigms kick in and kill them.

Although we as humans aspire for what's better, our brains prefer safety and stability, which resists change and leads to inaction. This feeling of being stuck is not unique to you, as we all experience this. The difference is that people like you and I seek the answers, and we invest in ourselves to make that change. We know that if we don't change something, we will still be on the same path and pattern of not getting what we want and in constant questioning. I applaud you for valuing yourself enough to take the time to read this book and make that change because we all know how incredibly difficult it is. But making the decision to do it is the first step, and you are well on your way to overcoming your paradigm because you have made it further than most.

> *"We have the power to forge our own path in life,*
> *so embrace this deep within and know that you are*
> *the creator of your own destiny."*
>
> *~ Jennie Lynn*

CHAPTER REFLECTION

Please take a moment at the end of this chapter to reflect on something that stood out to you. Record the greatest lessons you will want to remember so you can read these from time to time.

_____

_____

_____

_____

_____

_____

_____

_____

_____

_____

_____

_____

_____

_____

_____

_____

_____

_____

_____

_____

_____

_____

CHAPTER 2

STINKIN' THINKIN'

*"When we react, we lose control. When we respond,
we stay in control. By raising our awareness,
we are no longer prisoners of our past, but rather an
ever-expanding soul living our future.*

~ Jennie Lynn

In this chapter, I am going to share two examples of shocking research that were done which prove the unbelievable power of our thoughts. When I learned about these, my jaw dropped, and it immediately motivated me to change and cease the self-deprecating victim mindset.

The water experiment was conducted by Dr. Masaru Emoto in 1994, where he photographed water crystals that were frozen after being exposed to a variety of words and music. What he captured was nothing short of breathtaking. You will see the beauty of the first picture where gratitude and love were spoken to the water. On the left, you will see the distorted and chaotic picture of the water that was exposed to hateful and ridiculing words. The reason this is so significant is that our bodies are made up of approximately 60 percent water/fluid. So imagine how your thoughts are impacting your body and your soul and the language you use to communicate known as self-talk. For the first time ever, Emoto captured the astounding physical impact that our thoughts and intentions have on water.

"Thank you" on the left and "I hate you. You disgust me" on the right.

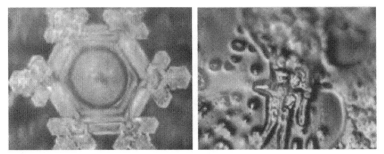

http://www.masaru-emoto.net/english/water-crystal.html

Dr. Emoto furthered this experiment by conducting the rice water experiment. He put rice into three glass containers and filled them with water. The first jar he expressed gratitude toward, the second he expressed hatred, and the third he completely ignored. He did this for one month, and the results were astonishing! The jar he expressed love toward fermented with a pleasant scent. The jar he expressed hatred toward turned black. The jar he ignored had rotted, and he concluded this was the most unfavorable of all three. It is scientifically proven as evidenced by this experiment that our thoughts are as real as light and sound waves and create similar waves in the universe that cause a positive or negative ripple effect. As you can imagine, how we treat ourselves and others with our actions, thoughts, and words can have a profound physical impact.

Dr. Masaru Emoto's Rice & Water Experiment

| "Thank You" | "You're an Idiot" | "Ignored" |

http://lionsgroundnews.com/the-power-of-mind-fake-chemotherapy-results-to-30-percent-hair-loss/

Another strong and powerful research study was done to exemplify the power of the placebo/nocebo effect and how our thoughts are so strong that they can impact us on a physical level. There are many studies that have been done, but this one was particularly distinguishing.

A double-blind study was done where a group of cancer patients was told they would all be given a chemotherapy drug that would induce hair loss. Half the group was given the chemotherapy drug, and the other half was given a placebo drug. The group that received the drug all lost their hair. A large percentage of the group that received the placebo drug lost their hair as well, simply by believing and expecting hair loss was a side effect of the chemotherapy drug. You may ask yourself how this is possible. In both the rice/water experiment and this chemo placebo experiment, they both manifest the incredible power and mind-body connection that our thoughts can have.

What you tell yourself, you actually believe, and what you repeat as beliefs into your subconscious actually materializes. It has a strong psychosomatic impact. These studies can show you the impact that your thoughts and paradigms have on you, and how important it is for you to learn and develop constructive patterns and positive thought processes. Without doing so, it will never be possible for you to receive what you truly desire. Be extremely careful with what you think because that is what you will believe. We don't necessarily control our thoughts, but we can control which thoughts we want to believe and reaffirm. Learn to ensure that you embrace the positive and reject the negative. The next time you think negatively or have a self-deprecating thought, remember these experiments and pictures, and train yourself to shift your thinking immediately to gratitude and love.

> *"Knowledge expands our awareness of our true potential but is useless unless it is acted up."*
>
> ~ *Jennie Lynn*

CHAPTER REFLECTION

Please take a moment at the end of this chapter to reflect on something that stood out to you. Record the greatest lessons you will want to remember so you can read these from time to time.

CHAPTER 3

RESULTS DON'T LIE

*"If you want to change your results – really change them,
forever – shifting your paradigms is the only way to do it.
When that shift happens, everything changes."*

~ Bob Proctor

It is very common for people to be in denial about their lives or they believe the lies they tell themselves; sometimes the truth hurts. However, despite any defense mechanism or denial, results do not lie, and the truth is the truth whether we agree with it or not. We get in life what we attract, what we are, and what we focus on. It is only when we take responsibility for our destiny and realize that we must make an internal shift to change what results we are getting in life that this will transform our reality. What we must do in life is realize that our emotions help us to recognize what vibration we are in. If we are feeling good, we are in the right vibration, but if we are feeling bad, we need to shift what we think so we can feel good.

Nothing in life is bad or good, but it is heavily influenced by our perception as we filter our experiences in life. Our paradigms control the frequency we transmit to the universe, as again, the subconscious mind is not under our control. Paradigms control our thoughts, which control our behaviors, which are then reflected in our results. We cannot attract anything we desire if our paradigms are not in vibrational harmony, which people often describe as feeling "stuck." We are all electromagnetic beings and a mass of vibrating atoms. We communicate through energy. Bob Proctor frequently explains that we are an "ocean of motion" and that the law of vibration declares that everything moves and nothing rests. Emotions are a conscious awareness of our vibration. Once you learn how to shift your vibration consciously to be in harmony with your paradigm, you will readily invite the universe to deliver what you desire like a magnet. Do you ever go out in nature and wonder why it is so calming? It's because the vibration of nature is in perfect harmony. As you discover yourself on a deeper level, you will truly appreciate what intuition really is. You will learn that the only advice or opinion you need is yours alone, and trust that your inner wisdom is there to guide you, and if you listen, your conscience speaks to you.

"Your results today are merely the reflection of your subconscious thoughts and beliefs from yesterday."

– Bob Proctor

I wanted to share one word of caution, as I mentioned that as you initiate some changes in your life, you will meet some resistance. This is due partly because our brain was designed with survival mechanisms, and while this inner voice speaks to us, we have to learn to recognize when we need to silence it and when to listen. For example, when you strive for a large goal or you're taking a risk, your brain interprets this as uncomfortable or a fear of the unknown, which sends a stress signal to the brain. Your brain will rebel, and your reaction might be to hesitate or over analyze. You can easily become paralyzed by this as your brain pleads with you to do what's "logical," which would be to retreat to a place of safety and comfort. Your brain will try to flood you with all the reasons why you can't or shouldn't, but when you know this decision will better your life, you need to focus on why you can and should.

We all know that to grow, we must make a sacrifice and be okay with getting out of our comfort zones so we can truly actualize our potential. The issue is that there is often a gap between what we know and what we do. While danger is real, fear is just an illusion that our mind creates that perpetuates worry. Those emotions do not serve us, and only attract to us what we do not want. This is the opportune time to shift that focus, to think outside of ourselves, as we raise our awareness to take conscious control and achieve the desired outcome.

One of the most crucial skills you can master in life is to make decisions. So many people don't know how to make decisions, so they ask other people who also don't know how to make decisions what they should do. Additionally, we get so caught up in whether or not we are making the right decision that we end up making no decision at all. It's okay to make the "wrong" decision, but again, there is no right or wrong because a decision we feel was wrong ultimately revealed what we don't want so that we can correct it. This is valuable feedback.

Again, learn to trust your inner wisdom as you connect your higher self. When you have an amazing idea, within good reason, you should take action before the primitive brain and paradigms have a chance to squander it. Most people get stuck wondering how they will do something when they should be focusing on why. When we are heavily motivated by a strong reason why we are doing something, it stretches our mind to conceptualize the resources and actions to bring that into reality. The bottom line here is that once we make a decision, we then create the need for the universe to respond. A common example of a money paradigm is if someone wants to purchase a home or a car, but they say they have to wait until they have the money. What they fail to realize is that they have no need for the money because they have not made a decision to purchase anything. Hence, it will never come. People often get frustrated because they think the law of attraction doesn't work, but it most certainly does if we produce the right signal.

Once we make the decision to purchase something as opposed to wondering how we will get the money, the universe will deliver the money to us in ways we had not even thought about. The results we get in life occur as a consequence of our choices and decisions. As you gain more of an understanding of your subconscious and your unique habits and mind blocks, you will be able to identify what you need to do to shift your thinking and your vibration to manifest the precise results you desire.

"Successful people make decisions quickly (as soon as the facts are available) and change them very slowly (if ever). Unsuccessful people make decisions very slowly and change them often and quickly."

~ Napoleon Hill

CHAPTER REFLECTION

Please take a moment at the end of this chapter to reflect on something that stood out to you. Record the greatest lessons you will want to remember so you can read these from time to time.

_____

_____

_____

_____

_____

_____

_____

_____

_____

_____

_____

_____

_____

_____

_____

_____

_____

_____

_____

_____

_____

_____

CHAPTER 4

BELIEVE TO RECEIVE

"There is a difference between wishing for a thing and being ready to receive it. No one is ready for a thing until they believe they can acquire it. The state of mind must be BELIEF, not mere hope or wish. Open-mindedness is essential for belief. Closed minds will not inspire faith, courage, or belief."

~ Bob Proctor

The reason most people fail when applying the law of attraction or give up on the concept is that they think that wanting something is enough to attract it. It is true that the desire is where it begins, and imagining and fantasizing helps it to manifest. However, most people are not aware of their paradigms, which act like a roadblock to them receiving what they desire. One of the most significant lessons I have learned is that if my paradigms are not in harmony with what I desire, I will never get it; wanting it or wishing for it is not enough. Go back and read that again because this was the biggest light bulb that went off for me. I struggled so long because I didn't know this, and it resulted in a great deal of frustration and discouragement.

To change the outside or alter what you receive, you need to change the inside, which is your energy and frequency. When you control the paradigms, you control the results, which is exactly what I practiced. Whenever I hear others talk about their success and how they achieved what they wanted or finally attracted what they desired, it helps strengthen my faith. I am so inspired when other people realize that it can be done because if they can do it, I can do it too, and you need to adopt this faith in yourself. You need to embrace limitless thinking and realize that abundance and all you desire is out there waiting for you. There is no shortage of resources. There is a shortage of belief or in connecting with the resources and desires so that is why you're reading this so you can learn the skills you need.

There was a point in my life where I was not a believer, and I got stuck at "how" and didn't understand all of this. But what allowed me to succeed was my refusal to give up. I needed to believe beyond all doubt I would get what I really wanted. You have to believe in yourself and the power of all of this. If other people can do it, you can too. Everything anyone has ever achieved in life started with a thought or an idea, and bringing it to fruition is a matter of connecting the energy and frequency. But the most common missing element is belief! It is challenging to believe all of this, but that is why you need to have faith. Train yourself to banish words like hope or maybe because those words don't serve you.

This is an all or nothing concept; there is no gray. The universe delivers with immense precision so once you understand this, be patient, and continue to specify exactly what you desire. You will get it. This is not philosophy or wishful thinking. This is physics, and these universal laws are as real and as powerful as gravity.

If you ever want to attract what you truly want, you have to remove the focus off what you don't want. Most people are in debt, and they are trying to attract wealth, but they have paradigms that are keeping them stuck. Their level of awareness and desires are not in harmony with their paradigms. You need to face your fears, or they will continue to rule your life. Fear is like praying for what you don't want to have happen, and wasting energy on this attracts the very things you don't want.

You need to banish all doubt, stop hoping, and start believing you both deserve and will get what you desire even though you may not know how. For so long, I struggled with that concept because my fears were controlling me, and I developed bad habits and thinking patterns. When you learn to dial in your focus with laser-sharp precision, and though you may not know how it will come to pass but that it will, the universe will get right to work on sending it to you. There is great power in what we focus on, because again, what you are thinking about you bring that to manifest.

We have an amazing mental faculty called the reticular activating system which helps us with sensory input and perception. It helps filter out certain thoughts so that we can focus on something specific as opposed to entertaining each and every thought that enters our mind. It is a very important component of our brain's cognition and allows us the ability to pay attention. We can only focus on so many things at any given time, but the most common example of the reticular activating system in motion is the car example. I encourage you to try this because it works! Think of a type of car model and color that you want. Once you put that thought into your head and choose to focus, you will see that car showing up left and right. You may have not ever noticed how many are actually all around you, but now that you specifically declared that intent, you start to see more of it.

The reticular activating system also helps process information between the conscious mind and the subconscious mind. This is how we speak to our subconscious mind and why it's so important to master this skill. What we think about – good or bad – manifests into our reality. We are the creators of our destiny. This is why you need to monitor your self-talk because you want to create good self-fulfilling prophecies as opposed to negative ones. When you live mindfully instead of mindlessly, you will learn to catch yourself thinking or saying things that you can correct.

For example, instead of saying the word "if" when referring to what you want to manifest, replace it with "when." Instead of saying, "I want," restate your intention with "I am" or "I choose." When you hear yourself saying, "I hope that does not happen," shift this focus to become a positive affirmation of what you do want to have happen. These small mental shifts really will amount to an enormous difference in your outer reality and results. Remember the power of your thoughts, and whether they are good or bad, the universe will respond to the frequency and energy you are emitting. If you find yourself feeling a low vibration or negative vibes, this is where you need to learn to shift this and train yourself back to positivity. This essentially is what controls your entire destiny. Believing that you're in control, that you have the power, and that you can change it at any given time is all fundamental. This is such an empowering concept, as there is an incredible power in belief and all the faculties of our mind.

"Everything is energy, and that's all there is to it.
Match the frequency of the reality you want, and you cannot
help but get that reality. It can be no other way.
This is not philosophy. This is physics."

~ *Albert Einstein*

Jennie's
3 STEPS TO GETTING ANYTHING YOU WANT

1. DEFINE what you want

2. DECIDE you will commit to doing whatever it takes to get what you want

3. DEDICATE yourself to taking action everyday to not only get that, but keep it

Don't miss out
on more free reports, updates and checklists
like this by subscribing here:
www.JennieLynn.com/Subscribe

CHAPTER REFLECTION

Please take a moment at the end of this chapter to reflect on something that stood out to you. Record the greatest lessons you will want to remember so you can read these from time to time.

CHAPTER 5

THE CHOICE IS YOURS

"There is both good and bad in everything according to the law of polarity. By raising your conscious awareness, you can train yourself to see the good. The choices we make dictate the consequences we face, and if we desire better consequences, our perception must shift to support better choices.."

~ *Jennie Lynn*

On any given day, we process hundreds of thousands of thoughts. If we entertained every thought that entered our minds, it would be chaos, and that is why we have a subconscious and a conscious mind. At any given time, we can choose what thoughts we will entertain and those that we reject. It takes some time to develop this level of awareness. We can choose thoughts that destroy or thoughts that empower. Whenever you feel yourself in an uncontrollable downward spiral of negative thoughts or fears, you simply need to shift your energy to focus on something pure like gratitude. You cannot be angry and grateful at the same time, and there is always something to be grateful for.

You get to choose whom you surround yourself with. Be careful of your energy and whom you spend your time with. It's all about quality. Pay attention to how you feel around people; do they inspire and energize, or do they drain and discourage? If you're the most successful person in your circle, you need a new circle because surrounding yourself with smarter and more successful people will push you to learn and grow beyond. We won't ever go beyond the people we spend the most time with because energy is contagious, and our environment is a strong influence on our potential. You need to learn to believe in yourself, and it helps immensely to be surrounded by others who believe in you as well. You probably recall learning about peer pressure or your parents warning you about hanging around with certain people who were a "bad influence." This is a similar concept in that we are a product of our environment and we need to learn to take conscious control of this so that it nurtures and inspires our desires.

A word of caution is not to ask for the advice of others. Learn to trust and listen to your inner voice. Again, most people don't think and are victims of their paradigms and limiting beliefs, and they will project this onto you. While they may offer well-meaning words, this will only confuse you in the long run. They are not subject to the consequences of your decisions, so ensure that you are not letting their paradigms and fears limit you. Also, do not fear making the "wrong" decision or you will end up in analysis paralysis. It is better to make a decision and find out that it is not what you wanted than to do nothing at all and stay stuck. We can always make corrections, and this is how we all learn, so don't be afraid of this. Successful people make a habit of making decisions quickly and changing them slowly if ever. Pondering about a decision too long will invite your paradigm to take hold, and you will rationalize, over analyze, and paint a picture of all the things that could go wrong and why you should not do it.

An example of this could be a boy who sees a girl he admires and wants to talk to her. If he doesn't act quickly, his paradigm may surface and give him reasons to doubt he is capable of approaching her. This is very common among people who are shy, and this in itself is a paradigm or fear that they reaffirm. At the end of the day, you're accountable for the decisions you make, so make them on your own, and learn to trust that you know what's best for you. Understand the power of a decision because once you decide on anything, those thoughts translate to frequencies to attract it into your life. Making any decision now creates the need for the resources that the universe will send, so if you get stuck or don't fully believe in your decision, you will send mixed signals to the universe, which can block you from receiving what you want. Consider if you want your life to change. You can look back on this moment a year from now, and you will have either remained the same, or you will have taken the action needed and realized how far you have come. Remember that we are a result of the choices we make, so if we don't like the results we are getting, it's time to make better choices.

"Remember, no more effort is required
to aim high in life, to demand abundance than is required
to accept misery and poverty."

~ Napoleon Hill

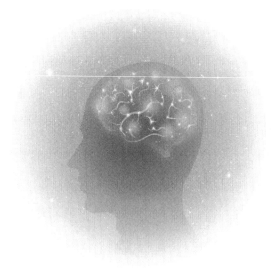

CHAPTER REFLECTION

Please take a moment at the end of this chapter to reflect on something that stood out to you. Record the greatest lessons you will want to remember so you can read these from time to time.

SECTION 3

A BLESSING
IN DISGUISE

CHAPTER 1

EMBRACE THE STRUGGLE

*"Sometimes we must accept that we may not always
get what we want, but our highest self intuitively knows
what is best for us, for our growth and fulfillment.
Don't resist, but rather embrace this."*

~ Jennie Lynn

It's easy to quit; it takes hard work and persistence to believe when you have every reason to doubt or give up. It takes courage to learn to trust again if you have been betrayed or had your heart broken. We must understand though that it is entirely necessary to know suffering to know peace. We need the opposite extreme to be able to recognize each experience. Keep in mind though that nothing is good or bad, but merely is what it is until we add meaning and perception. I once heard a motivational video from Les Brown, and it really helped me understand that I need to embrace the struggle and not curse it. Pain is a very strong motivator for change, and sometimes when you think that things are falling apart, they may be falling together.

"Sometimes we have to ask ourselves what's using my life. Heard a guy give a lecture one time that says, 'We are today what we were when.' And he was talking about the fact that we, to a great extent, behave, think, react because of some previous experience that we have had. One of the things that we know about life is that it is always changing. Sometimes you're up; sometimes you're down. Sometimes things go really well, and sometimes they don't. Sometimes you're happy, and sometimes you're sad. Now that's that thing called life. And when we begin to understand and know that, accepting that reality that we will never have things just on an even keel all the time.

You're going to have some ups and you're going to have some downs. But during those down moments, that's where the growth takes place. That's where the work is. People can feel good when they have their health, their bills are paid, they have happy relationships, the children are acting normal, and business is successful. Anyone could be positive then. Anyone could have a larger vision then. Anyone can have faith under those kinds of circumstances, am I correct? See, but the real challenge, the real challenge of growth, mentally, emotionally, and spiritually comes when you get knocked down. Somebody said that adversity introduces man to himself or woman. How you handle it, that's where the growth takes place."*

When I first heard this, it resonated with me because our character is really tested when times are tough. When life gets tough, I just tell myself it's another one of life's tests, and I refuse to fail. Now that I found my soulmate, we hold each other accountable and lift each other up. Despite how bad life may ever get around us, the fact that we have each other helps keep us grounded, and we can persevere through any obstacles. The lesson here is to understand that when we persist beyond our struggles, it makes us stronger and helps us realize and believe in our capabilities.

> *"When the time comes in life for you to make a change,*
> *the universe will make you so uncomfortable*
> *you will eventually have no choice. Our souls crave growth*
> *just as our bodies crave oxygen"*
>
> *~ Unknown*

*https://www.youtube.com/watch?v=UMd5W615Dbo

CHAPTER REFLECTION

Please take a moment at the end of this chapter to reflect on something that stood out to you. Record the greatest lessons you will want to remember so you can read these from time to time.

CHAPTER 2

THE BLAME GAME

"The universe does not discriminate, it merely responds to your frequency. Think negative, attract negative; think positive, attract positive. Whatever signal we put out in the universe, we will get back like an echo – this is an absolute law."

~ Jennie Lynn

A common mental barrier we face is feeling like the world is against us or that we are a victim. The universe never punishes us. It's not God's fault, or our parents', or our spouses'. The universe only responds to the frequency we tune in to, so if you're on a negative frequency, you'll attract negativity. If you focus on problems, you will attract more problems. You need to take responsibility for the consequence of your actions leading to your destiny. People are going to betray and hurt you, and it is natural to want to blame them and hold a grudge. All this will do is put you into a negative frequency and attract more of that negative feeling.

When you hold a grudge or blame someone else or something that happened, you give away all the power you have to take control of it. You will be a victim and a prisoner until you learn to let go. When someone does something hurtful to you, don't try to hurt them back or get even. Do not wish them ill will or hope that the law of karma will punish them because by sending out that negative energy, it will come back to you! Love is such a healing power, while hate and anger are so destructive and a waste of our precious energy. It is hard to forgive others and ourselves, but it is critical that we understand the consequences of failing to do this. It is the equivalent of keeping a wound open and never allowing it to heal.

One thing we need to be careful of is the temptation to give into our ego. Only when we transcend our ego will we truly be able to be so aware and in control that we intuitively know what is truth. Our ego, much like fear, is an illusion. Our ego cultivates selfishness and people who are offended by anything usually have a large and sensitive ego. It keeps us reacting in the same old way, when we should be responding and maintain control. When we abandon our ego, we have no need to be right or prove others wrong or argue. We discover our true self.

Our ego can often cloud our judgment and create friction in relationships. People often argue because they are not communicating or listening. They are not on the same frequency and they are not focused on the solution. Emotional intelligence is a skill we all must learn and embrace because we communicate with energy. When you can accept responsibility for things that happen to you and realize you played a part in attracting it, you claim your power to be able to do something productive with it. By looking for the bright side of anything bad that has happened or anyone's attempt to hurt you as opposed to giving away your power to a negative vibration, you embrace your liberation.

Remember that nothing is a waste of your time. If your experience didn't bring you what you wanted, it taught you what you didn't want. In life, we are going to make mistakes, and none of us is perfect. So do not expect perfection from others. Mistakes let us know that we are trying, and it will remain a mistake only if we do not take the lesson from it and ensure it doesn't happen again. Likewise, it is almost futile to regret anything in life because we make decisions for a reason and at the time we made it, it was exactly what we wanted.

So understand that nothing is a waste of time, and all experiences good or bad help mold us into who we are. It is sometimes natural for us to envy other successful people. I would frequently see other couples in love and be jealous of what they had because I wanted that too. This behavior was a bad habit which left me feeling poorer of love instead of feeling inspired by it. Feeling envy toward anyone for any reason is an insult to yourself, and it certainly won't make you attract what you want any faster. It is also lethal to compare yourself and your life to others. Most times we see someone who is successful and think they have it easy or just got lucky. But you don't know a person's entire story or the struggles they faced to get where they are. It's natural to want to judge the scenario, but focus that energy on yourself. You need to get off the pity pot and change that thinking immediately.

The reason we battle our own insecurity at times is because we compare our bloopers with everyone else's highlights. The lesson here is, to be honest with yourself and understand life is not a competition, so stop comparing yourself to others as a measure of your worth and success. We have all heard that the grass is always greener on the other side, but you should be so busy watering your own grass that you won't have time to waste looking at anyone else's. Life will tempt you with such things. With technology nowadays, anyone can post anything on social media and paint the picture of an ideal life, but they rarely if ever share their failures, so be realistic about this. If you want something badly enough in life, you will find a way to get it if it is important enough to you. If you don't act quickly enough, your paradigm will not allow you to take action, and you are bound to make excuses. The past is gone and cannot control you unless you allow it, so let it go and focus your energy not on the broken days of yesterday but on the gift of the present and promising future.

"There is a battle of two wolves inside us all. One is evil.
It is anger, jealousy, greed, resentment, lies, inferiority, and ego.
The other is good. It is joy, peace, love, hope, humility, kindness,
empathy, and truth. The wolf that wins? The one you feed."

~ Cherokee Proverb

CHAPTER REFLECTION

Please take a moment at the end of this chapter to reflect on something that stood out to you. Record the greatest lessons you will want to remember so you can read these from time to time.

CHAPTER 3

ROCK BOTTOM

"Embrace the fact that everything you have gone through both good and bad has molded you into who you are today – each and every experience was a part of your divine path."

~ *Jennie Lynn*

Throughout this book I've made mention to some of the times I struggled or seemingly failed. As an adolescent, I was shy, insecure, and I didn't have a healthy self-image. I grew up a tomboy and what I would consider an ugly duckling and a late bloomer. I never got asked to school dances or prom, and to be honest, that was okay because I had no interest in those things anyway. I was not the pretty, popular girl in school. I was the girl every guy was afraid of because I acted like a boy and had no interest in girly things. And that was okay until I started showing an interest in relationships. I had my heart broken a few times, and I internalized the pain and withdrew from being social and outgoing.

I went through a very dark time where I felt like I was in a deep hole with no way out. Life seemed pretty depressing, and it was hard to see the light at the end of the tunnel. It was so bad to the point that I felt life had no meaning unless I had someone to share it with. As desperate as I was for that loving connection with another, my attitude and thoughts were pushing it further away from me. There were some serious lessons I needed to learn. Many times I felt I hit rock bottom in life, like asking myself how much worse it could get. I was stuck in my own emotional prison.

When you think you're at the lowest point in your life, the good news is that it can only get better from there – unless you choose to stay there. What I learned from hitting rock bottom was that I was not paying attention to or aware of some patterns of behaviors that were driven by my paradigms. The universe kept sending me people and experiences to help teach me what I needed to learn, but I didn't understand and just got more and more discouraged. Again, life will keep repeating a lesson to you over and over until you learn from the mistakes. I know how incredibly difficult it is to believe and have faith when time after time, I wasn't getting what I wanted. I was tempted to quit, I wallowed in despair, and negative thoughts flooded my mind. But I had to fight those thoughts and choose to believe.

Life will constantly test you to determine if what you truly want is worth fighting for. Despite how hopeless any situation in life ever got, I always thought to myself that it could be worse. There are people much less fortunate than me, so I reflected more on what I did have and tuned into a frequency of gratitude. I found inspiration to persevere by learning about people like Thomas Edison, who refused to give up after failing nearly 10,000 times in pursuit of incandescent light before he succeeded. Think of how powerful and liberating is it to know that you can do anything you want in life, be anything you want if you silence the inner voice holding you back and tempting you to stay in your comfort zone.

Remember that for our results in life to change or improve, we need to change from within, and that requires a paradigm shift. People in our lives are either a mirror or a teacher. Sometimes we get so clouded in emotion and lament about what happened that we lose the lesson. Sometimes people were helping me recognize my behaviors even disguised in painful ways, but instead of being realistic, my ego got defensive. Instead of thanking these people and being grateful for the experiences which would help me learn and grow, I would just blame them and continue a vicious cycle of negative thoughts, which attracted more negative frequencies. This was a very bad habit I needed to learn how to stop. This was the paradigm rearing its ugly head. I eventually learned that anytime something "bad" happened, I always sought what it was trying to teach me. I pondered what I was doing that was attracting a frequency of what I did not want, and I would simply and purposefully shift. I made this a habit that has served me well to this very day. I learned that I am in control of my energy and became consciously aware of whether I was spending it productively or wasting it on nonsense. Now that I experienced what it felt like to hit rock bottom, I have corrected the bad behaviors that led me there, and I continue to take action to ensure that I don't make those same mistakes again.

> *"Rock bottom can become the foundation*
> *through which you now have the*
> *power to rebuild your life."*
>
> ~ *Jennie Lynn*

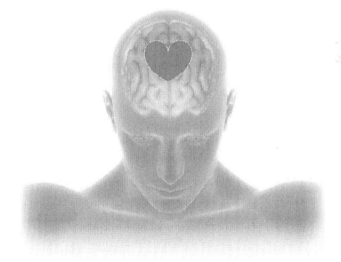

Jennie's
TOP 20 REASONS RELATIONSHIPS FAIL

1. Lack of self-love – if we truly loved ourselves we could never harm another. Also, we cannot love another until we love ourselves because this void is a self-seeking behavior.

2. Attachment. Craving love desperately instead of having love complement your life and detaching from the end result. People want to feel free.

3. Miscommunication – most people are not emotionally mature or consciously aware of their reactions, thoughts, and habits that sabotage their relationships. Effective communication and confidence are a critical foundation.

4. People ignore red flags and make excuses or try to force it to work. You need to spot an emotional manipulator or toxic person and know when to cut ties with someone as you as you know it's not a fit... and not feel bad or guilty about it.

5. You can't find what is meant for you if you keep clinging to what is not. When you know what love is, you will also know what it's not and you won't fall for superficiality and you will know what captures your heart and not your eye.

6. People are not their true selves and they wear masks so they fall in love with a façade of a person and that is temporary and when the real person surfaces, problems arise.

7. We go into a relationship thinking of what we can get instead of what we can give.

8. Not reconciling emotional baggage and fears from previous relationships and failing to check ourselves and identify that we could be the cause of our problems (ego) and not starting each relationship with a clean slate.

9. Disillusion – not appreciating what the relationship is because we are so preoccupied with what we think it should be.

10. Not actively learning what love is and who we are so that we know exactly what we want and also to know when we have found it. Failure to evaluate our results will cause them to continue repeating and we will face the same dilemmas until we change.

11. The two top reasons for divorce are: inability to effectively communicate with others and acting out of ego-driven needs, as well as conflict over money – neither of these were taught in school. We MUST actively learn these ourselves. Of course the obvious ones, lying and infidelity, are close in third and fourth.

12. Being jaded about love and relationships because we have been hurt and saying things like "love stinks". This is also similar to not being fair and realistic with your expectations and perceptions. Not everyone loves the same way or has the same beliefs, but you will find someone you're compatible with.

13. Having the victim mindset about anything instead of taking responsibility. Keep an open mind and learn a better way so you can live it. Be an optimist and a team player.

14. You also can't be tempted to jump ship the minute times get tough – that's another bad habit you need to break. There is a difference between knowing when a relationship isn't meant to be, but when you say forever, mean it.

15. Beware of destination addiction which is thinking that when you have what you want, then you can be happy and you can't be happy without it. The journey to our desires molds who we become and shapes our attitude.

16. Mind your self-talk. When you raise your awareness you will be able to eliminate self-sabotaging thoughts and habits and replace them with those that will serve you and create permanent desirable results.

17. Practicing daily gratitude and the art of presence with relationships so you not only find love but keep it. The honey moon phase can and should last forever. Any belief to the contrary is a lie you tell yourself and you will believe it. Break the cycle. Complacency kills and we are growing or dying, so learn to create, not stagnate.

18. Trying to control other people or change them into being what you want. If a person is doing their best, decide if that's what you want and if they do not want to change, then leave. Trying to force someone to change to please you is a recipe for disaster.

19. People who don't have confidence in themselves do not trust themselves. So they give their side of a story to a person they know who isn't qualified to give advice and who is not going to have to face the consequences. This is a big mistake, develop your intuition and let it guide you.

20. Insisting you must do this alone or rejecting the idea of having a coach/mentor can leave you feeling stuck, but only as long as you let it. A coach can fast track you to both identifying your destructive patterns so you can immediately remedy this and stop chasing your desires and instead learn how to easily attract them to you like a magnet. Sometimes you need to get out of your way and out of your own head and have someone connect the dots for you.

When I was at my worst, I wished someone would just tell me what I was doing wrong so I could fix it. I kept doing more of the wrong thing and ended up more hurt and discouraged which put me in a negative vibration and perpetuated more of what I did not want. If you want that love life of your dreams NOW, email the expert JennieLynn@JennieLynn.com, and let me help you!

CHAPTER REFLECTION

Please take a moment at the end of this chapter to reflect on something that stood out to you. Record the greatest lessons you will want to remember so you can read these from time to time.

_____

_____

_____

_____

_____

_____

_____

_____

_____

_____

_____

_____

_____

_____

_____

_____

_____

_____

_____

_____

CHAPTER 4

LIBERATION

"Attract what you intend, amplify what you desire, embody what you respect, and imitate what you admire."

~ Unknown

You probably understand by now, and more clearly than ever before, what drives our thoughts and actions. You are now fully aware of what paradigms are so that you can explore what they are within you and create new ones that are in harmony with what you desire. You may be wondering how to determine if you are a captive of your paradigm, and all you have to do is evaluate your results. Consider this saying, "How can you escape a prison if you don't know that you're in one?" Are you getting what you want? Do you have the body and the relationship or the career you desire? If you do, then you're doing it right. If not, you need to keep digging deeper until the paradigm surfaces and make some changes.

It helps to do this exercise of introspection in groups because sometimes we have blind spots that others can help us discover. If you do this in a group setting, make sure they are all people who understand this material and are not random people who have no idea about this information because it will confuse you both. Realize that you were born free and that life is both simple and beautiful. Over time and through experiences, we become chained down with limiting beliefs and become a prisoner of our minds. It will be an incredibly liberating feeling to be able to identify what is holding you back and finally be able to free yourself and live the life you desire.

This is something I struggled with for years, and I wrote this book to help you find the answers that I so desperately sought myself. I want to share my experiences so that you can find your freedom and live in the abundance we all deserve. It was not something I fully understood until after I finally received what I wanted. Now that I have much more understanding of what happened and what I needed to do to break free of those paradigms, I felt compelled to convey this all in a book and share my love story with you. Bob Proctor says that you cannot connect the dots looking forward, only backward. So understand that there are many lessons we can learn from our past and apply to our future. Understand that you didn't arrive at where you are in life overnight, and this is all a process that you need to be patient with to have optimal results. I have faith in you that you will soon find the answers and be able to free yourself from the burdens clouding your life so that the path to your desires becomes crystal clear. It's a good idea to set realistic expectations and embrace this as a process.

Anyone, including myself, who has mastered the information I reveal here, has read many books and invested deeply in him or herself. It's often not a journey we can or should make alone, which is why it is so powerful to mastermind and network with others. It is also why we need mentors and gurus who inspire us because when we study others, we absorb their knowledge so that we learn much faster than we ever could on our own. We can extract the knowledge they have spent a lifetime gathering so that we help program our minds with valuable information.

When I was in some of the most chaotic times in my life that I describe, I could not see other things clearly nor get out of my own way. I thought I could do it all on my own, but I was not aware I was in a prison of my mind and in a vicious battle with paradigms. I needed the help and guidance of a seasoned mentor who could show me the way. There is no quick fix to this, and I spent a lifetime developing beliefs and paradigms that won't vanish overnight. After all, even Einstein states that "A problem cannot be solved on the same level of thinking that caused it." This is why it's imperative to invest in your mind and discover yourself so you can see the whole picture. Mentors and coaches help empower us to be our best selves, and they hold us accountable when fears and obstacles appear. I am happy to provide such guidance, as I have invested in my training as a world class Proctor Gallagher Mentor and Consultant. I am certain that if you tell me what you want, I can show you how to get it. I offer one-on-one and group/corporate coaching where I will help you discover the infinite abilities you already have. I strongly believe in the Chinese proverb, "Give a man a fish and you feed him for a day; teach a man to fish and you feed him for a lifetime." You will find my personal contact information, social media, and website information at the end of this book.

"Each morning when you look in the mirror, make a habit of asking yourself if what you do today will take you closer to or further from your goal. You cannot change your reflection without first changing yourself – the same applies in life in that we cannot change our outside reality until we change our inner thinking."

~ Jennie Lynn

CHAPTER REFLECTION

Please take a moment at the end of this chapter to reflect on something that stood out to you. Record the greatest lessons you will want to remember so you can read these from time to time.

_____

_____

_____

_____

_____

_____

_____

_____

_____

_____

_____

_____

_____

_____

_____

_____

_____

_____

_____

_____

SECTION 4

LEARN THE ART

CHAPTER 1

STAGES OF LEARNING

"When a baby learns to walk and falls down 40 times,
he never quits or thinks to himself or herself,
'maybe this isn't for me.'"

~ Unknown

I absolutely love that quote because it puts things into perspective of how easily we give up on something. Babies aren't even aware of what quitting is, so it is not an option, and they inherently know they need to learn to walk by watching their parents. Imagine for a minute what it would be like if babies actually quit learning how to walk and crawled for the rest of their lives. The next time you're struggling to learn something, remember this quote and let it inspire you to be patient and keep going.

In reference to learning, few people ever voluntarily study love or educate themselves as we never really receive any formal teaching about it growing up. Engaging in relationships just appears to be something we experience, and most paradigms will reinforce the patterns, so you never think beyond what you do and what happens. Come to find out, most people don't know what they don't know, and I was one of those people. To understand how we learn, you will see there are actually four stages of competence:

Unconscious incompetence: You don't know what you don't know
Conscious incompetence: You become aware that you don't know
Conscious competence: You purposefully learn what it is you don't know
Unconscious competence: Learning and skills becomes second nature or we are skilled without even knowing it*

* https://www.mindtools.com/pages/article/newISS_96.htm

The chart above exemplifies the stages we often go through when we learn. Sadly, though, most people never make it anywhere near stage four; the few that do work hard to get there or are lucky enough to be there and not know it. Only a very small number make it to stage three. Some people make it to conscious incompetence, but they don't take action to learn what they need to in order to change. Unfortunately, the majority of people never make it beyond unconscious incompetence because they think they have life all figured out, and "when you think you know, you simply will not grow." That is the epitome of the vice grip a paradigm has on a person and where they get stuck.

Most people you see everyday aren't really living. They are merely existing or surviving and not living life on purpose. They just deal with each day not giving much thought to what they want in life. They pretty much have a routine, and because they have been deeply programmed, they never question anything and merely follow the crowd. Some people who are inquisitive are always thinking there must be a better way or more to life, and they never settle. The most successful people in life are those who can adapt and learn to think for themselves.

In school, I was given the superlative of most inquisitive because I was always asking questions. I loathed school though because I always felt like I was being forced to learn information and take tests on things I felt I would never use. It actually made me hate learning and reading, and as soon as I graduated college, I never wanted to look at another book again.

I am glad that I developed a love for reading and learning again because I was now able to pursue these on my own and choose what I wanted to read. There is no end to the number of books out there, and I almost feel as if there is not even enough time in a day to read all the books that I want. The knowledge offered in school will teach you what to think but not how to think. They don't even teach you how to make decisions, which is why most people fall victim to analysis paralysis. This is when they contemplate a decision so much that they can't decide and ultimately end up stuck and take no action. They don't teach you about wealth, or relationships, or life in school which is a shame.

When people finish high school or college, they think they're done learning, and this is a huge mistake. It is one thing to be educated and successful in school, and this may land you a decent job. But if you want anything in life, you need to learn what drives your thoughts and actions. We learn by repetition, and for you to be an expert at anything, you need to practice it habitually.

Dedicate yourself to become a student for self-development. Find successful people who have done what you want to do, and follow them, and learn from them. There is a whole world of knowledge out there. It is one thing to read or learn something that inspires you, but if you never put it into practice and reaffirm the lesson, your paradigms will not change. You want to aim to reach unconscious competence so that you are so successful with your skills that they become second nature. Learning is an art and a process, so be patient and love the journey so that it transcends into a natural and worthwhile adventure of self-discovery.

"In order to learn, we must open our mind. Those who are close-minded are often overly confident and therefore cannot learn more, whereas, those who lack confidence fail to believe they can – finding balance between either spectrum is the key."

~ Jenny Lynn

CHAPTER REFLECTION

Please take a moment at the end of this chapter to reflect on something that stood out to you. Record the greatest lessons you will want to remember so you can read these from time to time.

CHAPTER 2

WE ARE WHAT WE THINK

"We are shaped by our thoughts; we become what we think. When the mind is pure, joy follows like a shadow that never leaves."

~ Buddha

Whether we accept it as fact or not, we are spiritual beings who communicate by means of energy frequencies. Similarly to the law of gravity example, denial of any truth does not change that it is fact. Every day we choose our state of mind, our state of health, and our environment. Our attitude is the greatest influence on the energy we both emit and attract and is the one thing we can control in life. What goes on in our mind affects the lens through which we process life, and sometimes that lens needs to be adjusted. This is again a learning process you will shape and develop throughout this book. I went through a distinct shift in my life in 2013. I specifically remember just feeling at peace, and confident, and comfortable. It's as if I was living life at a different level of awareness, almost like I woke up and shifted off autopilot. I later learned that this is known as a spiritual awakening. It usually surfaces after periods of suffering as we learn to shed the false layers and masks and realize who we are and what our purpose is in life. It was an incredibly liberating feeling I will never forget.

Our thoughts are more powerful than we can ever imagine. Thoughts turn into words, which then turn into habits, and they form and shape what we perceive as reality. We believe what we tell ourselves, so if you are always putting yourself down and reaffirming your inferiority, you'll continue to believe this and never excel. Remember Dr. Emoto's water experiment next time you think unkind thoughts toward yourself. The most important lesson from this entire book is that for you to attract and receive anything you desire, you must love yourself. You must have positive paradigms and believe you are worthy of what you are attracting. If you are not getting what you desire, it may be that it's not meant to be, but more likely that you are not completely in harmony with your paradigm. Remember that there is an abundance of everything out there. We just need to tune into that frequency like a radio station.

Our paradigms keep us in patterns of limited thinking and even control our income and our potential. You will never travel or even think beyond them until you both identify and change them. For example, people make $80,000.00 a year because they don't know how to make that in a month. If they knew how, they certainly would be. Many people get stuck because they don't think or believe they are capable of more. Their paradigm may make them question, "Who do you think you are?" They get stuck because they don't know how they could achieve such lofty goals and soon give up. The idea that we could travel to the moon was once just a thought and far-reaching idea. But a few dedicated people who refused to give up succeeded in making that thought and dream an incredible reality. Most people don't stretch their minds. It is very difficult to do this until you learn what a paradigm is, and then you really discover how much more there is to life. We can attract anything we want, and we will get it as long as we align our paradigms and believe. If you don't ever ask for it, you certainly won't get it, but you can't just wish for it and expect it to appear. You have to allow your mind to expand, and allow yourself to believe in the abundance all around us. Our imagination allows us to dream and fantasize, and it helps connect us with our deepest desires. Remember, you have the immense power to change your life and yourself simply by changing your thoughts.

"Great minds discuss ideas. Average minds discuss events.
Small minds discuss people."

~ Eleanor Roosevelt

Jennie's
5 Steps to Becoming a More Desirable YOU

1. Get in shape, be fun, get organized, and be ready for love.

2. Define what you have to give and offer your current/future partner.

3. Give it your all, 100%. Love requires more than a lukewarm heart – you need that burning desire.

4. If you lack confidence or any skill you need or desire, dedicate yourself to learning it immediately.

5. Have the right attitude. It's the only thing you can control and you will filter out any negativity and be honest and objective.

Don't miss out
on more free reports, updates and checklists
like this by subscribing here:
www.JennieLynn.com/Subscribe

If you have not visited
www.MagneticLove.com,
now is the time to claim your free bonus gifts,
but they are only available for a limited time as part
of the official launch celebration!

CHAPTER REFLECTION

Please take a moment at the end of this chapter to reflect on something that stood out to you. Record the greatest lessons you will want to remember so you can read these from time to time.

CHAPTER 3

AN EPIPHANY

"Success consists of going from failure to failure
without loss of enthusiasm."

~ Winston Churchill

Sometimes we think we know what is best for us, but the universe knows better. It listens not to our words or lies we tell ourselves but to our intent! You cannot fool the universe no matter how much you lie to yourself or deny certain truths. Change your thinking to always look for the positive or bright side of any situation. Whether we believe it or not, everything in life happens for a reason. There are no accidents. While the lesson may not always be immediately apparent, there is a reason and a lesson behind it, and if you pay attention close enough, it will be revealed. Have you ever gone through a breakup when you had your heart set on someone only to find out later that it was actually a good thing you're not with them because they are a mess? I will give you an example of this. A man I was dating broke off the relationship, and I was heartbroken. I could not imagine myself with anyone else, and it was as if my life was shattered. It was very hard to move on when I was clinging to this relationship. I eventually did move on, and years later I found out that this person would not have been a good match for me, despite how much back then I felt sure of it. The universe helped me dodge a bullet because that person was not my soulmate, and at that age, I had no idea what love was all about!

There were many other break-ups I had to go through and learn lessons the hard way. There were relationships that would end, and I would fight for them or get so angry at the man who broke it off. I eventually learned that if someone wants to walk away from me, I need to let them go. It was not a reflection of the fact that I was unworthy, just that the relationship wasn't meant to be, and I later learned why. If at any time you're forcing a relationship to "work," it's already over, so let it go. I was also a giver, and I always seemed to attract takers. I eventually learned to recognize the red flags and not make excuses for people's bad behaviors because I deserved better. I needed to set the tone for how I would be treated. You should never have to convince someone to stay with you. Never chase love because if it isn't given freely, it isn't worth having.

Sometimes I stayed in a bad relationship because I felt that ending it was a failure or quitting, and I was an optimist. I would often feel bad breaking up with someone because I would fear hurting them. I learned though that it is more favorable to be honest about my feelings than fear them. I should not be thinking for another person or worrying what they will feel like and end up over analyzing and fearing something that has not happened yet and may never happen. Being honest with someone even if you know they may perceive it as hurtful like a breakup allows them to experience what they need to learn and grow. So be honest, and don't rob them of that experience. You're responsible for your emotions, and they are responsible for theirs, but in any case, do your best to be genuine about it.

A very valuable lesson I learned was that no one could hurt me without my permission, and I cannot hurt anyone either. Think about that for a moment. We allow people to hurt us when we react to a painful stimulus. We always have the power to reject a behavior whether it was meant to harm or not; it's a matter of protecting our energy and being aware of this. We are very quick to respond to anything and often get defensive because of our egos and paradigms. There is a quote by Victor Frankl which is very powerful as he states: "Between stimulus and response there is space. In that space is our power to choose our response. In our response lies our growth and our freedom." Again, life is a sum of our perceptions, and this is heavily influenced by our paradigms as well as our attitude. The law of polarity states that there are both good and bad in all things, but we get to choose what we see based on our perception. Choose to see the good in all things, and you will feel your world change.

The greatest shift for me was that I realized I was just jumping randomly from one relationship to the next making the same mistakes because I hated being single and alone. That was not love at all; that was desperation. I would stay in the few relationships I engaged in even if they were far inferior to what I deserved because I feared being alone. I didn't love or respect myself enough to stay single and wait until I met a worthy fellow. Most often I would just say yes and hope for the best and just find out it was just another guy telling me what I wanted to hear and being on his best behavior only to have his true colors shine through. But this was my fault for attracting the wrong people and for the wrong reasons.

The cycle was repeated over and over. I finally realized that it was a big mistake to not only attach almost all my worth to being in a relationship as well as expect another person to be the reason for my happiness. This was because if I didn't have a relationship, I was surely feeling unworthy and being single meant unhappiness. I had come across a quote by Yoda which states that you should "Train yourself to let go of anything you fear to lose." There was also another quote by Buddha which states, "You only lose what you cling to." I certainly had a lot to lose, and I lost myself because I was clinging to relationships and at the same time suffocating them. Instead of acting out of love, I was acting out of fear. I feared that I would end up alone my whole life or that I would never meet that one great guy who would make all my dreams about love come true. We all know that feeding fear is like praying for what you don't want. I wasted a lot of time focusing on the wrong frequencies, and it took a great deal of introspection and affirmations before I was able to break that paradigm and bad habit.

Sometimes we experience difficulty letting go of our suffering because we have a fear of the unknown, but we inadvertently accept suffering that is familiar. When I first realized this, it really hit me because it is so true. But it was a sad reason to stay in a failing and unfulfilled relationship. Once I told myself I deserved better and it was not selfish or unreasonable to expect better, I was able to attract that. Once I mustered the courage to end a bad relationship, I was able to let go of what was not meant for me and make room for what was. I wasn't going to settle for just anyone who asked, but I was ready to meet the man of my dreams and believe he existed.

"Once you make a decision, the universe shifts to the precise frequency to make it happen."

– Jennie Lynn

CHAPTER REFLECTION

Please take a moment at the end of this chapter to reflect on something that stood out to you. Record the greatest lessons you will want to remember so you can read these from time to time.

SECTION 5

MANIFEST YOUR DESIRES

CHAPTER 1

THE BIRTH OF THIS BOOK

I wanted to share with you the story of how this book went from merely being an idea to being written in a matter of weeks. This book would never have been possible if I had given into my limiting paradigms. I wanted to describe what inspired me to write the book and the series of events that took place leading up to having it published and into your hands. It all started when I made the decision to invest $10,000.00 in myself to accompany my fiancé to meet Bob Proctor and Sandy Gallagher on December 4, 2016. At the time, that was a lot of money, but I overcame a paradigm and decided to do it because if I told myself I didn't have the money, I never would. But if I decided to go, the money would come, and it did.

During the Matrixx event, I was fortunate to meet Peggy McColl and learn of all her success as an author and a bestseller coach. I had my eyes set on other goals, so when she gave her presentation on her coaching programs, I was not planning on writing a book. The last night of this Matrixx program was December 9, 2016, and we were all invited to Bob Proctor's house for dinner. My fiancé and I were talking to Bob about how we met through the law of attraction. Bob was commenting on how simple it is to attract anything you want in life, including a love partner. He stated that love is a frequency that we tune into. It was at that moment that I felt instantly compelled to write a book about soulmates and our love story. I asked Bob if he could write the foreword, and he delightfully agreed. It was exciting, but I had no idea where to start. The one thing I did though is dedicate myself to this goal, fully believing in my capability, and I took action immediately.

The next morning, I started thinking about what I was going to use for the title of the book. About twenty-five different names occurred to me, and they were decent, but I was waiting for a special one to move me. Finally, something made me think of a magnet, and I have no idea why. I thought to myself, *that's it. That's going to be the title, Magnetic Love.* I could not think of a more appropriate title because it already encompasses an insinuation of attracting forces and, of course, the book is about love. I then proceeded to identify a good subtitle. Chasing is hard work, time consuming and offers no guarantee. Mastering our ability to attract what we desire requires much less time and effort, and when performed in harmony with universal law works precisely. "Like Attracts Like" perfectly explains the magnetic relationship between the law of attraction and the law of vibration.

The next step was to connect to the expert in the field, Peggy McColl. Bob Proctor said to do exactly what he says and exactly what Peggy says, so I listened. Both of them are amazingly successful in their fields of expertise and life, and their reputations precede them. I would highly recommend Peggy to anyone reading this who wants to write a book and become a best-selling author.

I contacted Peggy about my idea and wanted to make sure it was viable, and she agreed it was, so I hired her on December 12, 2016, to help coach me through it all. This was another expensive investment, but I didn't even think twice about the money because I believed in what I was doing and that it would amount to more revenue. Imagine if I had stopped because my paradigm was more attached to the money than the value I would get from this program to help make my book a bestseller.

With Peggy's guidance, I secured an editor and a company to help me self-publish the book. The next step was to make my book as real as possible, so I developed a mock book cover indicating that it was a bestseller. This was basically my book as part of my vision board, a display that I could look at each day and connect with the energy needed to make it all manifest. I also wrote down on a goal card that I was happy and grateful to be a *New York Times, Amazon,* and international best-selling author by a specified date in 2017 and how much revenue I expected to generate. I set a goal to be done writing my book by the end of 2016.

Thoughts kept flooding my mind, so I started to write them all down in a jumbled mess. As I was listening to Peggy's seminars, I began to learn how to organize all the information, so I made six sections. I identified them sequentially and started to categorize the information where it was most suitable. By the end of the day, I had six pages of content ideas written, and now I was ready to start writing. I was determined to write this book in record time, probably because I'm very competitive and driven. I was able to beat my deadline by about seven days, and I finished writing the book by Christmas Eve. That was about ten days from start to finish. I was shocked at how fast this went from being an idea to, in a matter of weeks, my very first book.

This is how to maximize the law of attraction, and the universe likes speed. I had so many breakthroughs and revelations even as I wrote this book. I found myself really following my own advice and revisiting all the lessons I ever learned in life. I never reflected on my past this much or delved this deep into my psyche. It was as if my mind was continually expanding, and I could feel it! I could feel my energy rise and the immense excitement I felt every time I talked about my book. This is how I know I am following my passion; this is how I want to feel and how I know I am in vibrational harmony. I thought to myself that this is what it must feel like when you win the lottery and that I wish I could bottle up and store that feeling. It continues to amaze me the enormous power of my mind and how the answers were continuously revealed to me.

One of the most important lessons in life is to master the art of remaining calm and not ever losing my cool. A good analogy I like to use to best exemplify this is muddy water in a jar that represents a storm. If you shake it up, it becomes cloudy and murky, which represents chaos and desperation. During this storm, we can't see a way out, and we stress ourselves out by trying to figure out how. But when the glass is calm, and the dirt settles, the water becomes clear and settled. And after a storm, there is usually a beautiful rainbow. When the mind is quiet, this is when we find clarity, inspiration, and all the answers we seek. This often creates an emotional high when you break past barriers and survive the storms and realize just how much you're capable of enduring.

I remember this one breakthrough I had where I started to feel like I was overflowing and had so much abundance; it felt heavenly. I had so much energy that I really didn't know what to do with myself. I have invested so much of my soul into this book so that you can learn to unleash this power within you. I truly hope that this inspires you to follow your passion and believe that anything is possible. I discovered so much about myself, and it is so amazing to be able to share it with you and help you to feel this incredible sense of vitality, peace, and surrealism.

Another lesson I learned is that I no longer see money as scarce and something I should cling to. I see it merely as green paper that gets me the things I want most. I believe that money is abundant, and I just need to connect with how I am going to get it. I stopped complaining about how anything is too expensive because that only reinforces a poverty mindset. My paradigms about money have shifted exponentially. I learned to make decisions quickly and not allow my paradigms to talk me out of them. The more I made this a habit, the easier it became, and the birth of my book is all proof. This whole experience has completely changed my life. Realizing the amount of damage I was causing to my soul and my body with a perfectionist paradigm became apparent to me, and overcoming this has been the most incredible change I've ever made to heal my relationship with myself and unlock true abundance in life. Bob Proctor told us that it's not being in the right place at the right time that makes people lucky and successful. It's that they are aware they are in the right place at the right time. It finally clicked, and it was clear to me what I needed to do, and I fearlessly made my dream into a reality.

Now that I have developed mindfulness in everyday living, I catch my mind wandering sometimes, and I consciously shift back to a positive vibration. I learn not to entertain any thoughts that do not serve me or cause me worry or stress. Every day now, I tell myself I will able to make a living both helping people and doing things I love, and that is exactly what has manifested. As I create this book, I've been writing the story of my past, and I discovered the amazing power I have to write what I intend for my future and how I am manifesting my destiny as we speak. Perhaps the most profound revelation is that by virtue of spending two months writing this book and immersing myself in both new and old lessons I've learned, I experienced this massive transformation as if all that collective power combined created a massive quantum shift. All of this material was swimming in my mind repetitively for two months, so much so that it really saturated in my subconscious mind to help me overcome my paradigms and help me heal.

That is precisely what I teach as part of Bob Proctor's curriculum, and it really was just a serendipitous bonus to my goal to complete this book. I constantly look back in awe of how much my life transformed. In the next few chapters, I will break down for you this entire process to simplify it and make it easier for you to assimilate this into your life.

CHAPTER REFLECTION

Please take a moment at the end of this chapter to reflect on something that stood out to you. Record the greatest lessons you will want to remember so you can read these from time to time.

_____

_____

_____

_____

_____

_____

_____

_____

_____

_____

_____

_____

_____

_____

_____

_____

_____

_____

_____

_____

CHAPTER 2

GOALS: IT ALL STARTS WITH A VISION

"All we are is a result of what we have thought.
The mind is everything. What we think we become."

~ Buddha

Everything in life that manifests was once a thought that was consciously acted upon. Ideas and thoughts cannot manifest unless they are connected to the frequency that causes them to potentiate. For you to attract anything you desire, you need first to explore exactly what you want. You have to create a clear picture in your mind with no ambiguity. Most people never stop to consider what they want, let alone the thought or possibility of actually getting it. This is sadly why most people live an unfulfilled life and merely survive and exist. It is truly sad to witness so many people that are prisoners of their paradigms, and they don't have the capability to expand their minds.

Anything I ever wanted in life started with a dream and a goal. I aspired to pursue a career as a nurse, so I took action and enrolled in college and graduated. I aspired to work in the operating room at the best hospital in the country, Massachusetts General Hospital. I met the right people who helped me achieve this goal, and no matter what obstacles arose, I kept my focus on getting this desire. When I was growing up, I was the ugly duckling and shy, insecure young girl. I always dreamed of one day being pretty or even becoming a model. That seemed like a far-fetched goal when I could not walk in high heels and didn't even know how to apply makeup! I never gave up on my goals, though, which were always driven by deep passions and convictions. Not only did I become a professional model, but my love for health and fitness led me to another goal of achieving professional status in natural bodybuilding. I now hold three pro cards in figure, physique, and bodybuilding. I always dreamed of being on the cover of a magazine and being an esteemed writer, so all of these dreams came true because I had an unwavering desire and spirit.

One of my strongest qualities is that I am relentless, and I have been able to achieve anything I set my mind to do. I learned to break free of previous limits and connect to the frequency of my desires. I loved myself and believed I was worthy of these goals and dreams, and the universe responded. My paradigms almost held me back from writing this book because I had never written one before and I didn't know how I was going to do it. But as soon as I was committed to the decision, the inspiration came, and the universe delivered the people and resources I needed to make this dream a reality.

There are three types of goals. There are easy goals, which you can achieve because you already know how. There are goals that you can reach for that you think are possible. Then there are goals that you really want but are what you would consider almost a complete fantasy. You need to learn to make more of the latter two types of goals if you ever expect to expand beyond your current limits and paradigms. When we aim to achieve goals for things we have never done before, it empowers us to learn and stretch ourselves to connect to solutions. It is in pursuit of these goals that we grow, such that actually getting what we want is merely a bonus. Be picky about what you want, and don't settle for less. Dream big, and allow your imagination to flow. This is the time to get creative! Explore what you're truly passionate about in life.

Most people have not even given much thought to what they want in life, let alone to write it down. If you ask them what they want, they'll say they don't know. They are stuck in a box they cannot think outside of, and therefore never push those boundaries or live a fulfilling life. They don't create their lives; they simply operate out of paradigms and circumstances. If you don't know what you want, you can find out what that is by identifying what you don't want and thinking about what is the opposite of that.

Understand that it's good to have an idea of what you want, but don't be too rigid to the point where you miss the universe sending you what is meant for you and you don't see it because it is not exactly how you intended it to be or when. When we appreciate life as it is, we no longer demand that it ought to be what we think it should be, and this is the real path to peace. We may not achieve all of our goals, but they provide targets for us to aim for so that we have a place to start. It's okay for your goals to change as you evolve.

Furthermore, our ideas do us no good if they are only kept in our head, and this is why you need to get it on paper and also so you don't forget it. This is why repetition is key: we only have so much memory capacity, and we remember more of what we write ourselves. You need to be specific about precisely what you want. It is important for you to feel emotionally connected to your goal as well. You need to identify when you want to achieve your goal because the universe knows no concept of time, so attach a specific date. If you want a certain income level, then list how much money you want to make in an exact dollar amount. Pay attention to the energy you feel when thinking about your goals. Some of your goals might scare you and they should. You are challenging your paradigms, and you need to persist beyond any barriers and get creative.

Whenever you decide on what your goals and desires are, you need to write them down. I made the mistake of just thinking that the universe knew what I wanted, and I knew what my goals were and didn't need to write them down. Plus I was too "busy" in the rat race of life, like most people, to stop and take the time to reflect on what I truly wanted. I used to be guilty of this, but I find that so many people are so disillusioned by society and focusing on surviving day to day that they don't spend any appreciable amount of time to slow down and mindfully manifest. Then they wonder why they end up where they don't want to be and getting results that are anything but what they want. We really do create our lives, and instead of letting life happen, we can map out our destiny every day! We need to get off autopilot and start driving. When you write a goal down on paper, you have now made an intangible thought tangible and one step closer to being real. I have made it a habit to rewrite my goals each day in a journal because the more I remind myself of them, the more I focus and connect to the emotions of how they make me feel. I am speaking to my higher self and my subconscious mind and planting the seeds of what I want to grow. My soul is speaking to me, and I am speaking to my soul. I just start writing all the things I am grateful for, and it really reminds me how blessed I am.

I find it peaceful and liberating to put these thoughts down on paper and reflect on them because there is always so much going on in my mind. I am reaffirming the things I want to manifest as if I already have them. Remember that if you don't have a map and a plan for your life, you'll surely end up somewhere you don't want to be. Having clearly defined goals helps keep you on track and allows the universe to guide you.

"The most successful people didn't wait until they were "ready" to do something. Any delay is often an excuse our paradigms gives us to keep us stuck where we are – if the circumstances aren't right, you have the power to change that."

~ Jenny Lynn

If you would like to learn more about
how to build more wealth and
create permanent financial freedom, visit
www.CashConsciousness.com
for a FREE report for you.
Hint: They didn't teach this in school.

CHAPTER REFLECTION

Please take a moment at the end of this chapter to reflect on something that stood out to you. Record the greatest lessons you will want to remember so you can read these from time to time.

_____

_____

_____

_____

_____

_____

_____

_____

_____

_____

_____

_____

_____

_____

_____

_____

_____

_____

_____

CHAPTER 3

THE VISION BOARD

*"Vision creates the final destination – it's the coordinates
we preset into our mental GPS system so that every turn we take
leads us to our goals – without a vision, you
may wander endlessly in the wrong direction.."*

~ *Jennie Lynn*

A vision board is a poster of pictures or affirmations that display what your goals entail. This is your board of dreams and desires. It is essential for you to get a clear picture of what you desire so your message to the universe is clear. By looking at pictures repeatedly, we help connect to our desires in a unique way, and this behavior acts as a daily reminder of the energy we need to summon. Our minds think in pictures so when you have an idea of what you want, get a picture of it immediately and capture it. Your vision board can have your dream job, your dream car, your ideal body, your dream house, and the man or woman of your dreams. The pictures should paint a clear and vivid picture of exactly what you want. Some examples would be a couple kissing or holding hands. It could be a picture of you in a wedding dress or tuxedo perhaps. It could be positive and inspirational quotes about love. You want to specify both in your goals and on your vision board that you are attracting your soulmate. Have fun painting this whole picture. Put a picture of your favorite love story or movie that you hope your love life will emulate.

I am so glad that I finally made a vision board, which was one of the missing elements to making my dreams manifest, so I cannot stress enough to put some dedicated time and thought into this. Dreams fascinate me when we go to sleep, and our brain creates stories of things have never happened, or I meet people I have never met. This is your chance to dream while you are awake, intentionally and purposefully. Your imagination is such a powerful force because it is how you learn about what you truly want in life and love. Your imagination creates excitement within you that helps you connect to the vibration you need to create to attract your deepest desires. The anticipation and feelings of you actually receiving what you want help make it even more real.

This is precisely what you need to do and create in your mind those future memories, where you fantasize and create the mental pictures that you can bring into the present. You almost have to stage it in your head like it's a movie, and rehearse it over and over. If it's a job you want, picture yourself having a successful interview, write an acceptance letter, and determine the salary you want. If it's a car you want, go and test drive it, and take a picture of yourself in it and place that on your vision board. If you want your dream home, picture yourself in every room, envision yourself shaking hands to close the deal, and put pictures of it on your board. If it's your ideal body, picture yourself running along the beach and how confident and comfortable you feel. I find that meditation and visualization are so powerful, and there are videos and exercises you can do to help you truly connect in a state of altered consciousness to those desires. Really feeling those emotions helps you connect to that frequency and make it feel real, which then potentiates the universe to deliver it to you. Ultimately, you must have a clear and specific idea of what you want so when you find it, you will know.

*"Your vision will be revealed only when you look into your heart.
Our power emanates from within – never look outside
of yourself – all you will ever need is within you already,
you just need to become aware of it."*

~ Jennie Lynn

CHAPTER REFLECTION

Please take a moment at the end of this chapter to reflect on something that stood out to you. Record the greatest lessons you will want to remember so you can read these from time to time.

_____

_____

_____

_____

_____

_____

_____

_____

_____

_____

_____

_____

_____

_____

_____

_____

_____

_____

_____

_____

_____

_____

CHAPTER 4

REPETITION, REPETITION, REPETITION!

"The first law of learning is repetition. We must study and make learning a habit – this is the key to success."

~ *Jennie Lynn*

The easiest way to attract yourself to the frequency which will connect you to your desire would be to embody what you want. If you want to have good friends, you must first be a good friend. If you want a faithful, loving partner, you need to be loving and faithful. Remember that life is an echo, and what we put out comes back to us, so ensure that your energy and desires are pure and clear. When you are thinking of what you want, you must reaffirm this desire as if you already have it, so instead of saying, "I *want* something or to be something," say, "I am grateful that I *have* or I *am*." The universe will respond by keeping you in a state of wanting, and then you won't take any action. You have to bring it into the present, and this will make it manifest. Once you receive a few of the things you desire, you will be amazed at how magical but yet real this all is. You will see that you can learn to connect your energy and attract what you want with magnetic precision.

Most people don't truly believe in the law of attraction because they think it's merely wishful thinking and getting lucky. That's a paradigm holding these people back. Paradigms are incredibly difficult to change, and the only way they can be changed purposely is through constant spaced repetition. For anything to be true, you need to believe in it first. Some people don't believe in soulmates, and it's no surprise they may never find theirs. We don't all want the same thing, and there is plenty of abundance for what we all desire.

Each day, you need to make it a habit to express gratitude as you read your goals. Do this at the beginning of each day, and the energy you need is sure to follow. You should even rewrite your goals so that you can speak to your subconscious, which is the most powerful way to create new beliefs and habits. Look at your vision board every day, and fantasize about how you are feeling now that you have those things. Feel this deep in the core of your body and soul. Remember that your ability to attract what you desire depends on your ability to believe you will get it. One mistake I made is that when I was single and lonely, I kept thinking irrationally that being in a relationship would magically solve my problems. I could not feel happy unless and until I received what I wanted.

"Be cautious of something called
destination addiction – just like love, happiness
comes from within – not as an end goal.
Until you surrender the idea that happiness is
somewhere else, it will constantly elude you."

~ Jennie Lynn

This was the wrong frequency because the universe responded to me being lonely and ungrateful, so I wasn't getting what I wanted. I was getting more of what I didn't want. I should have been practicing gratitude and happiness so that I would attract a relationship where I could both bring and share happiness. If you don't appreciate what you already have, you will never appreciate when you have more; therefore, the universe will not send you what you desire until you change this. You need to figure out where you are so that you know where you are going and you're on the right path.

With time and dedication, you will develop a deep level of self-awareness and intuition. I really like a quote that Bob Proctor pointed out to me by an anonymous person that states: "When we pray we are talking to God, and when we use our intuitive faculties, that's God talking to us." The more you practice this, the more it will become second nature, and what you desire will flow to you more easily.

"Repetition is the preface of learning, the catalyst of action, which makes it the sculptor of our achievement and ultimate destiny."

~Jennie Lynn

CHAPTER REFLECTION

Please take a moment at the end of this chapter to reflect on something that stood out to you. Record the greatest lessons you will want to remember so you can read these from time to time.

SECTION 6

EVERLASTING LOVE: STORIES OF INSPIRATION

CHAPTER 1

THE LOVE STORY OF PEGGY MCCOLL

Peggy McColl is a world-renowned expert and a *New York Times* best-selling author, speaker, and mentor. She is known as "The Millionaire Author Mentor and Bestseller Maker." She and I met in December 2016 at a Matrixx seminar event in Canada with Bob Proctor. I was so inspired by her success, and I have always wanted to write a book but didn't know where to start. It was destiny for us to meet to make this book possible, and I am honored that she was happy to share her unique love story about how she attracted her soulmate.

Peggy explained to me that it was important to convey where she was in life and what led her to ultimately attracting her soulmate. When Peggy was getting divorced, she realized and became aware of this paradigm that was causing her to sabotage her relationships. She came to the realization she did not feel worthy of love, and this was causing relationships to fail. She expressed how incredibly painful it was, not that her marriage was ending but that she would be spending less time with her young son, and that divided time is something she would miss. She felt compelled to explore this feeling that she was not worthy of love, which she discovered was deeply rooted in her childhood. Once she became aware of this, she was finally able to take action to do something about it. She developed a technique called "my power life script," which she had practiced diligently every day for the past two decades.

Basically, she wrote her life script of what her life would be like and all the things she wanted. She talked about her health, her relationships, her business, her finances, her dream home, and everything that was important to her. She wrote it so that when someone else read it, they would be amazed at how incredible her life was and she intentionally used emotionally charged and powerful words and reinforced the paradigms she needed to bring this to life. She wrote things like, "I am worthy of love. I am loving. I am giving. I deserve love. I have a wonderful relationship with my significant other," and she reaffirmed this over and over. She even recorded herself reading it and listened to it every day for years. She stressed that repetition is how we create new beliefs, and as she kept listening to this, she eventually was able to believe what she was saying and truly love herself and attract all these desires.

Peggy described the man of her dreams and what the relation-ship would be like. As time went on, it became clear to her and, more importantly, she felt as if she had already experienced this. It was as if what she wanted was already here. Once she made the decision that she was ready for love, it was about two weeks later that she met the man who is now her husband. Peggy had decided she wanted someone in her life. She didn't get out much or go to social events and was not intrigued by the thought of dating sites. Someone told her she'd better do something because it wasn't likely he would come knocking on her door. Peggy asked, "Well, why not?" She was confident that he would show up the way the universe intended him to and she would not know how. Funny enough, though, he did come knocking on her door! She had met this gentleman while walking their dogs one day. He knew where she lived and decided to stop by and ask if she could provide a favor. He was going out of town for business on short notice and needed someone to watch his dog for the day, and Peggy gladly agreed. When he came back to retrieve the dog, she invited him in for a coffee. This was the beginning of a wonderful relationship where they dated and were married a year and a half later.

Peggy explained to me that this would surely not have happened if she had not gone through the life script and affirmations daily. She is now grateful that she was able to attract her soulmate and they get to live a wonderful life together. I asked Peggy what it felt like when she met him and how she knew he was the one. She said she just knew because it felt exactly like what she described in her life script. It was natural, there was no forcing, no conflict of emotion, and it was almost like she just intuitively knew. There was no confusion around it though it was not instant, but she was certain, and so was he. She recalls one of their first dates where he was talking about politics and the news because he was a pilot. He made mention of the fact that they are so different. He stated that as a pilot, he has a plan for everything. He said that, on the contrary, if she decides to go anywhere, she just goes and doesn't know how she will get there. She stated that what made them a strong couple is that despite their differences, they had a great deal of mutual respect. She said they had the same values and were people of integrity. She said they were equally responsible, ethical, and honest.

They made a commitment to themselves, and they stuck to it. Family was always important to them, and they always had their priorities straight. She felt that they were both good people by nature, and their love for each other grew and continues to grow because they deeply respect each other. She stated that when you love someone, you don't try to change each other. That never works, and you need to learn to love who you are and who they are. It is a lot easier than people think to attract love and their partner, and people often try to force it rather than let it unfold. Forcing anything is never a part of the process. If you get frustrated because it's not working, you will push away what you want unknowingly. She stressed it is imperative for people to be patient and follow the teachings, and they will work. She summarized by saying that we can have all that we desire if we just believe in it, change our paradigms, and just have fun and love life.

CHAPTER 2

THE LOVE STORY OF YOURS TRULY

Throughout my entire life, there is nothing I have wanted more than to meet my soulmate and spend the rest of my life sharing the joy and making memories together. I had been reading many books about love and had a folder of love quotes on Facebook, and I came across a particular photo, and something really *clicked*.

You're a spiritual being in human form. Sometimes you simply desire to connect with a soul who feels like home.

SOURCES: https://mulpix.com/post/985616776193607654.html

The quote on this picture really resonated with me because I agreed that falling in love feels like coming home. It's comfortable, secure, warm, and safe. Home should be in the arms of your soul mate. I had been practicing the law of attraction, but this picture inspired me to finally make a vision board, so I printed it out and found some other quotes and pictures online of what I wanted in my soulmate and ideal man.

A few days later, on August 5, 2016, I had finally made the decision to give online dating another try. I didn't get out much to meet people and, because I was young and did not want to have children, I wanted to be able to filter out and meet people of like interests. I signed up for a six-month membership and wished for the best. I immediately started to get in-boxed messages and spent most of the day responding to some people. I woke up the next morning to tons of new messages. As I was going through them, I received a very charming message from a man named Brian, so I checked out his profile and decided to write him back. Long story short, we felt a compelling connection, so we exchanged numbers and didn't waste any time talking on the phone to get to know each other better. He was very attractive and had a lot of diversity and character. We both had a lot in common, which we found out through long conversations, and we felt a strong intellectual mutuality. We learned that we both studied the universal laws and law of attraction and had the same values.

It was a refreshing feeling to meet him and learn of all his success and altruism. A few days after he messaged me, I mentioned to him that it may sound crazy but that he was everything I wanted that I put on my vision board. I told him I only joined Match a few days ago, and he said his jaw dropped. He said that he joined Match a few days ago, August 5, the same day I had. He said I was the first person he messaged. He said that a week prior, he built a vision board too and had written three pages listing all the qualities he wanted in his soulmate. He said he did this with his businesses but never did it for a relationship, and he wrote down that he would meet his future wife in 2016. We were both amazed to learn of this. How cosmic was it that we both joined Match the same day? This was surely no accident, but it was destiny that we met. Thank God for Match.com! We felt incredibly blessed, and it made meeting even more special. We planned to meet each other a week later.

He wanted to make it special and have it be over a weekend. At first, I agreed because I was head over heels and felt comfortable. But then, what I know now as my paradigm started to surface and I over analyzed the situation. I started to remember certain rules about what not to do on the first date. I was going to have to tell someone I was meeting someone new so that I would be safe in case something happened. What would they think? I wanted this to be as special as he planned and envisioned. I decided I was going to chance this and believe I would be safe. It was hard to silence all the fears about what others would think and stop worrying needlessly. [Full disclosure: whenever you are meeting someone new, I highly advise you to prioritize your safety and use caution, by meeting in a public place and establishing trust first.]

I'm glad I listened and agreed to the weekend date. Brian picked me up at my home in a limo. Each day leading up to this, I envisioned what our first embrace would be like, and we already agreed we owed each other a nice long hug and kiss. It's funny because kissing is usually something reserved after a few dates, if ever, and most times, it's awkward as to when it's appropriate. When I opened the door, I was overwhelmed with excitement and our first hug felt like home just as I had imagined, and it was the best kiss ever. How was it possible to feel so strongly for someone I had only known one week and had just met? Just like each relationship before, I got all excited and enamored except this was different. It was real. There was no awkwardness or guarding or fears about trust. I felt like I knew and trusted him already, and that's hard after your heart has been broken so many times, and I promised I would always go slower the next time. But I decided to throw out all the rules and start a clean slate and do what I felt was natural. I was able to feel comfortable and be myself around him, and we adored each other.

We spent the whole limo ride to dinner singing and talking and just staring into each other's eyes. We went to Davio's at Foxborough

Stadium and had a lovely dinner. We met a couple there that was celebrating their anniversary, and they just seemed so distant. Brian and I got right up and decided to slow dance in the middle of the restaurant, and we asked them to join and they wouldn't; how sad. We left there and went via limo to Foxwoods Casino where we danced all night to some amazing electronic music. You would think we had been together for years the way we danced and celebrated this first date. It was the most thrilling and intoxicating feeling ever.

I felt so full of life and a wave of energy I had never felt before. It was so powerful to connect with this unique frequency, and it was the feeling my soul always craved. We took the limo home back to his house and just fell asleep in each other's arm. I was so glad I made the decision and trusted I would be safe. We woke up the next morning and just cuddled and appreciated the wonderful gift of each other's presence. I felt like I had won the lottery. We went back to Foxwoods for the day for a pool party and danced and relaxed and enjoyed the beautiful summer day. The next day he drove me home, and it was painful to part ways. But I knew I would see him again soon, a few days later. When we met again, we were talking, and he told me he loved me, and this was only four days after we met. I was overjoyed and told him I loved him back. I gave him the key to my heart at that time. One of my tattoos on my inner ankle is a heart with a lock box, which I got because I always felt I had to guard my heart, but now Brian had the key, and he opened up my belief in true love, and I know with him I feel safe and protected.

Over the next few weeks, he told me I could move in if I wanted. Of course, I agreed because I didn't want to spend any more time away from him than I already had to. He told me that if I had been scared away after a first date like that or how he said love so soon or invited me to move in within weeks, he would have known I was not the one. But we both knew that we were soulmates. It was an instant connection. The attraction between us was magnetic, and we were magically in love and inseparable. We just connected on every level, physically, mentally, spiritually, and intellectually. We loved each other unconditionally, the way love ought to be.

I celebrated the fact that a twenty-nine-year search and struggle was finally over, and I've never felt more relief in my life. I never wanted anything more in life than to find my soulmate, and he was finally here! I almost could not believe it! A few months later on his birthday, we were all out to dinner on vacation in Punta Cana, and he was giving a toast and said he wanted me for his birthday. He got down on one knee and presented a beautiful ring, and we declared our love forever there. Each day our love grows stronger, and we express gratitude and count every blessing. We learned that we both had used the law of attraction to find each other. Every relationship prior had been a learning experience but one step closer. We both believed in and were ready for true love. We are partners in love and business and everything in life. We cherish the gift of our love and how fortunate we are, and we work hard together and support each other's dreams. There is no greater feeling in life in our opinion than to have your soulmate. Everything beyond that is a luxury.

We are still amazed at how fast we connected and how quickly we knew we were destined for one another. It's rare that two people are on the same page and feel the pace is appropriate and they get along so well. I love the fact that Brian makes me feel comfortable being my real authentic self. He also makes me feel fearless because he supports my dreams wholeheartedly, but he also keeps me level and helps me strive and stretch myself to be the best version of myself. It's sadly rare these days to find true love that lasts forever, but when you find it, you keep it and cherish the gift. I don't ever look back, and the past does not matter anymore. I don't care how long it took me to find him because I know that this was the right time and that we both had finally tuned into the right frequency at the right time to find each other. I realized that I must have finally done something right, and when it was revealed to me, all I wanted to do was share it, which inspired the compilation of this book. I found home in Brian, and he found home in me. We are completely devoted to each other for eternity, and my intention is that everyone who reads this book will have an unparalleled love story of their own.

CHAPTER 3

FLEX YOUR LOVE MUSCLE

*"Perhaps the strongest muscle in our body is our heart.
I can think of no other muscle that never rests until we die,
which can heal after it is repetitively broken, and offers an infinite
supply of love – what a miraculous design when you ponder this."*

~ Jennie Lynn

I hope that as you finish reading this book, you continue to study it intimately and live what you learn. I hope that you have discovered the power of your thoughts and how you can finally take control of them to live the life you desire. In order for you to attract your soulmate and the relationship you desire, the first step is to love yourself the way you would like others to love you. Love is an incredibly wonderful gift.

Build a life, and attract a love that you want, and believe that it is all unfolding. Celebrate as if what you want is already here, and imagine how amazing it feels. Falling in love is an emotional roller coaster, and a paradigm that most people have is that "the honeymoon phase won't last forever." I am going to tell you that the honeymoon is not a phase at all. The honeymoon feeling is just the beginning and will last as long as you want it to. Love should be a wonderful journey, and every day should feel as amazing as the day you connect with your soulmate. Again, love is a skill like any other, and for you to be able to master this skill, you must practice this daily. Remember anytime you're not manifesting what it is you want, you're likely focusing on its absence and not its presence. You already have everything you desire, you just need to become aware of it. Your heart is a muscle, and when we don't use our muscles, we lose them. When you do find the love of your dreams, continue the loving actions that united you both, because if you are persistent, you will likely to get it, and if you are consistent, you will keep it.

Please share this book and profound teachings with everyone you know. Not many people are taking initiative like you have because they are stuck in a prison of paradigms that they are not even aware of yet. Anne Frank states that "No one has ever become poor by giving," so spread the gift of love. Be that vehicle for them, and help us show them there is a better way. It has been an amazing privilege to help you learn and grow, and I sincerely applaud you for taking control of your destiny. I encourage you to practice gratitude daily and be patient with yourself.

Count your blessings because when you are thankful for what you already have, the universe will continue to reward you with more and more things to be thankful for. This is precisely how the law of attraction manifests in your life. We are limitless beings, and the only limits we have are the beliefs we choose, so choose abundance, and choose love. Overcome the fears and paradigms that are standing in the way of your dreams, and discover that you have everything you need to succeed. It may seem illogical to read this book again and again, but I encourage you to not only read this book, but study it repetitively.

As you expand your mind, you will surely extract more and more each time you revisit the wealth of knowledge in these pages and as your perception matures. This is why I had you write down the most important lessons you learned from each chapter so that you can go back and bookmark those pages and remind yourself of those lessons from time to time for continued inspiration. Remember that the best investment is in yourself, and to have a better life, you need to feed your mind worthy information from both people and books. Love the art of learning, and share it with everyone you meet; you never know how much you can change a life with one simple act of kindness. To be able to share this book with the world would require efforts much greater than just my own, so if you felt a great impact reading it, please share it with your friends and loved ones. I wish you all the love and blessings you truly deserve as you discover and attract a wildly magnetic and magical bond with yourself and deepest desires. Everything you want is waiting for you to simply tune into the right frequency. All you need to do is believe.

Congratulations on reading until the end of this book, and realize that this is just the beginning of an adventurous new way of life. Take action on all you have learned, and do not let any go to waste as you build the life of your dreams. Have an attitude of gratitude, and realize that our reality depends on the quality of our thoughts. Your soul is perfectly divine and yields a goldmine of universal power. Continue this learning journey to expand your mind even further, and you will soon attract the most magnificent days of your life and create memories that you will cherish forever.

> *"Love will elude those who chase after it while failing to invest in who they are as a person. The better person you are, the more love is attracted to you by virtue.*
> *Start with love, then apply this concept to anything you desire, because it is already yours."*
> *~ Jennie Lynn*

Here's to your happily ever after.

AFTERWORD

People often ask me, what is the most valuable lesson that I have learned that made the biggest difference in my life and my success? I love this question, but people are often surprised by the answer. The answer is: "It isn't what I have learned that made the difference... it is what I have done with what I have learned that has made the difference."

The fact that you are at this point in the book, and have read these materials, separates you from the rest. You have demonstrated that you are a doer. I believe in you. Something drew you to this book and the promise of the book. Know that you are in the right place and the answers you seek are contained within these pages.

And now I have a question for you: What will you do with this fabulous information that you have now obtained from the author of this book? Learning isn't enough. Studying isn't enough. Understanding isn't enough. For transformation to occur, you must DO something with these materials. My recommendation (if you haven't done this already) is to review the book again and highlight all the recommendations, and act today. Put these brilliant ideas to work for you.

The opportunity for you to take your life to a new level exists right now. You hold the key and are in the driver's seat. Where will you go? What will you do? What do you choose? If you could have, do, or be anything, what would you choose? One of the most powerful questions I have learned is the following: What would you love? This is a great starting point question (for setting intentions), and this is a great question to ask yourself when you find you are in a dilemma, at a crossroad, and don't know where to go or what to do. What would you love for you... for your life... for your family?

You may want to consider getting an accountability partner. Find someone who is like-minded and study this book together. Set intentions, and hold each other accountable. Support each other in a positive manner. There was a study done by Brigham Young

University several years ago that said that when you set intentions, create your plan, act, and report to an accountability partner, your chances of success are in the range of 95 percent.

About thirty-eight years ago, I read a book that changed my life for the better, but it wasn't the book that changed my life; it was following through on the recommendations that changed my life. That was the starting point. I have read hundreds (if not thousands) of books, written several myself, and been in the study of personal development actively for close to four decades. And my life has changed in only glorious ways and continues to do so. My wish for you, and I know the author's wish for you, is only success... victory in loving yourself, happiness in your relationships, fulfillment in health, money, freedom, and anything else you desire. There is a goldmine of wisdom in this book, and it is time to start releasing the greatness that is within you.

~ Peggy McColl, *New York Times* Best-selling Author
http://PeggyMcColl.com

RECOMMENDED READING

Think and Grow Rich – Napoleon Hill

The Five Love Languages – Gary Chapman

Four Agreements – Don Miguel Ruiz

The Art of Living – Bob Proctor and Sandra Gallagher

You Were Born Rich – Bob Proctor

Be a Dog with a Bone – Peggy McColl

How to Win Friends and Influence People – Dale Carnegie

Power of Intention – Wayne Dyer

You Can Create an Exceptional Life – Louise Hay & Cheryl Richardson

The Secret – Rhonda Byrne

Don't Sweat the Small Stuff in Love – Richard and Kristine Carlson

YOU 2 – Price Pritchett

The Power of Your Subconscious Mind – Dr. Joseph Murphy

WOULD YOU LIKE TO MAKE MONEY HELPING OTHERS LEARN ABOUT *MAGNETIC LOVE*?

If you know any school, non-profit organization, club, or cause that could really benefit from *Magnetic Love*, please kindly send me an email at JennieLynn@JennieLynn.com and send me the details and your contact information. I will generously reward you with a bonus for the referral depending on how many books are ordered.

SHARE YOUR LOVE AND GET REWARDED

Please Don't Keep Me A Secret!

I hope *Magnetic Love* exceeded your expectations.

Please help show others the way to love!

I am interested in your feedback and
care about your experience.

Please submit an email to me and tell me about your story at
JennieLynn@JennieLynn.com
and receive a FREE bonus gift from me.

This is my way of saying thank you!

WHERE IN THE WORLD IS *MAGNETIC LOVE*

Take a picture of yourself with the book and upload it to
the *Magnetic Love* facebook page at
www.facebook.com/magneticlovebook
and instagram **@thelovegenie** and **@magneticlovebook**.
One lucky winner each month will be selected to receive a private
coaching session with Jennie Lynn. Make sure to
hash tag **#magneticlove #thelovegenie** and tag all your friends!

ABOUT THE AUTHOR

Jennie Lynn (Hogue-Laurent) was born and raised in Southern Massachusetts. Jennie pursued her college education to become a registered nurse and has been practicing for the past seven years. She is also a fitness fanatic, and has been a successful professional model, and earned worldwide triple pro card status in natural figure, physique, and bodybuilding. She began her writing career as a magazine editor, and her articles have been published in and on the covers of *Natural Gainz Magazine, Natural Mag International, Muscle Sport Magazine,* and *Be Legendary Magazine.* Jennie is also a relationship expert, artist, mentor, speaker, and holistic health coach. Jennie Lynn is the co-founder of Matrix Success Network, which offers customized elite business coaching as well as individualized leadership and results driven, paradigm-shifting programs. She and her husband are among the top worldwide consultants in collaboration with legendary thought leader Bob Proctor and the Proctor Gallagher Institute. Her passions include nature, traveling, learning, and business. She ventured into entrepreneurship in 2016 and happily manages several other businesses with her husband, Brian.

Contact Jennie Lynn: www.JennieLynn.com
Email: jennielynn@jennielynn.com
Phone: 508-330-6217

Photo: Domenic Trapassi

Please subscribe to my Youtube channel for ongoing updates and webinars and inspiration: www.Youtube.com/C/JennieLynn

LET'S STAY CONNECTED THROUGH SOCIAL MEDIA!

Author Facebook Page:
https://www.facebook.com/jennielynnlovegenie

Magnetic Love FB Page: https://www.facebook.com/MagneticLoveBook

Facebook Fan Page Athletic: www.facebook.com/jennielynnlaurent

Instagram: instagram.com/magneticlovebook
Instagram: instagram.com/thelovegenie
Instagram: instagram.com/mizfitjennie

Twitter: www.twitter.com/mizfitjennie
Twitter: www.twitter.com/jenniethegenie

Photo: Ian Zagaglia

**Please request to join my private online community
for more exclusive updates, ongoing expert advice,
and to mastermind with other magnetic lovers.
Search for the group on facebook: MAGNETIC LOVERS.**

WIN WITH JENNIE LYNN! Subscribe today!

What can you gain from claiming your FREE subscription to my email newsletter?

1) FREE expert advice

2) Bonuses & discounts

3) Insider life tips/hacks and freebies

4) Exclusive & unique wisdom

5) Motivational & inspirational content

Visit **www.jennielynn.com/subscribe** to start winning!

MATRIX SUCCESS NETWORK
JENNIE LYNN AND BRIAN DALMASO

matrixsuccessnetwork@gmail.com (508) 330-6217

~ We would love to hear from you ~

ARE YOU READY TO DISCOVER YOUR TRUE POTENTIAL?

Take full advantage of a proven system that can FAST TRACK you to what you desire most.

We have done all the trial and error so you don't have to!

Our mission is to monumentally improve and enrich the lives of our audience on a global scale through individualized paradigm-shifting programs. We both empower and facilitate our valued clients through carefully calculated content provided by Bob Proctor and Sandy Gallagher from the Proctor Gallagher Institute. Through our elite coaching simulation, we aspire to guide our clients to raise their awareness to align in harmony with their highest selves and most coveted goals while achieving all levels of wealth and abundance. Being among the top inner circle Proctor Gallagher Consultants globally, we mentor thousands of clients and businesses toward limitless success and unparalleled results.

ACKNOWLEDGMENTS

There are so many individuals who I would like to thank who have helped mold me into the person I am today. First and foremost, I would like to thank Brian Dalmaso for choosing me to be his wife and partner in life. I could not have ever dreamed of a better match and soulmate and husband, and he is the most significant blessing I have ever received in my life. I would like to thank my parents, Gail and Lenny Hogue, for raising me in a nurturing environment and supporting all my dreams. I am grateful for all of my family, Brian's family, and friends who have stood by me and proven their devotion. Also, "Mikey", my Aussie brother and cosmic twin who I met along this journey and is a testament to the mission of this book which is love and light.

I am grateful for each and every person I have met and with those whom I've had relationships because we all learned from each other, and I don't regret my past. I send out love and gratitude to all my coaches and teachers who shared their knowledge with me along the way. My spiritual mentor and friend Rick was the first person to introduce me to the law of attraction and a whole different dimension and level of awareness in life, for which I'm eternally grateful.

I would like to thank everyone who made this book both possible and an amazing success so that I can help and inspire billions of people to change their lives and enjoy all the gifts life has to offer. I am grateful to Peggy McColl for helping coach me on how to become a best-selling author and guide me along this journey. I am grateful to Judy O'Beirn and the Hasmark Publishing team for editing and publishing my book as well as Anne Karklins who helped design the cover and interior graphics and also Anik Singal and the Lurn Nation family for helping me accelerate my business and skills in the internet industry and in my entrepreneurial endeavors. I would like to thank Steve Harrison and his Quantum Leap program and coaches for helping me achieve far more than I ever thought I could.

I am grateful to Bob Proctor and Sandy Gallagher who gave me the wonderful opportunity to work with the Proctor Gallagher Institute where I gained the confidence to write this book and pursue authorship. Ever since I saw the movie *The Secret* at the age of fifteen, I've been studying Bob Proctor, and I never thought I would ever meet him, let alone have the privilege to be part of his legacy and teach through the institute. For anyone who does not know who Bob is, he is a legend in the personal development industry and a master of the universal laws as a global thought leader. He is an inspirational speaker and author who has dedicated his life to teaching others how he turned his life around and became a multi-millionaire running a global business with virtually no education. If I had not gone to meet him at the Matrixx event, I doubt my life would have changed to the degree it did. I have been so blessed to have had many unique experiences and privileges in life including the opportunity to study the universal laws to live the life of my dreams and the freedom to pursue my destiny.

The Literary Fairies

we make your literary wish come true

Jennie Lynn

has partnered with

The Literary Fairies

who have a mission to give to those who have
experienced an adversity or disability an opportunity
to become a published author while sharing
a story to uplift, inspire and entertain the world.

Visit TLF website to find out how YOU
could become a published author or where
you can help grant a literary wish.

More details provided at
www.theliteraryfairies.com

Made in the USA
Middletown, DE
14 July 2017